CREATION
and the
COSMOS

A Poetic Anthology Inspired by Nature

edited by tara caribou

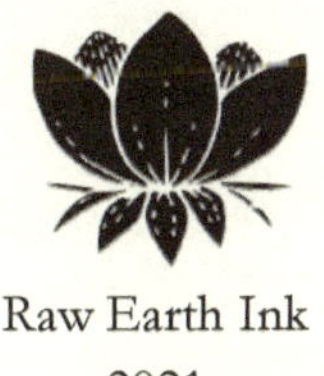

Raw Earth Ink
2021

This book is a work of poetry and art.

First paperback edition March 2021

Book and cover design by tara caribou

ISBN 978-1-7360417-4-1 (paperback)

Published by Raw Earth Ink
PO Box 39332
Ninilchik, Alaska USA 99639
www.raw-earth-ink.com

Table of Contents

Introduction

"An artist must possess Nature. He must identify himself with her rhythm, by efforts that will prepare the mastery which will later enable him to express himself in his own language."

~Henri Matisse

"Those who contemplate the beauty of the earth find reserves of strength that will endure as long as life lasts. There is something infinitely healing in the repeated refrains of naute—the assureance that dawn comes after night, and spring after winter."

~Rachel Carson

"Nature is not only all that is visible to the eye… it also includes the inner pictures of the soul."

~Edvard Munch

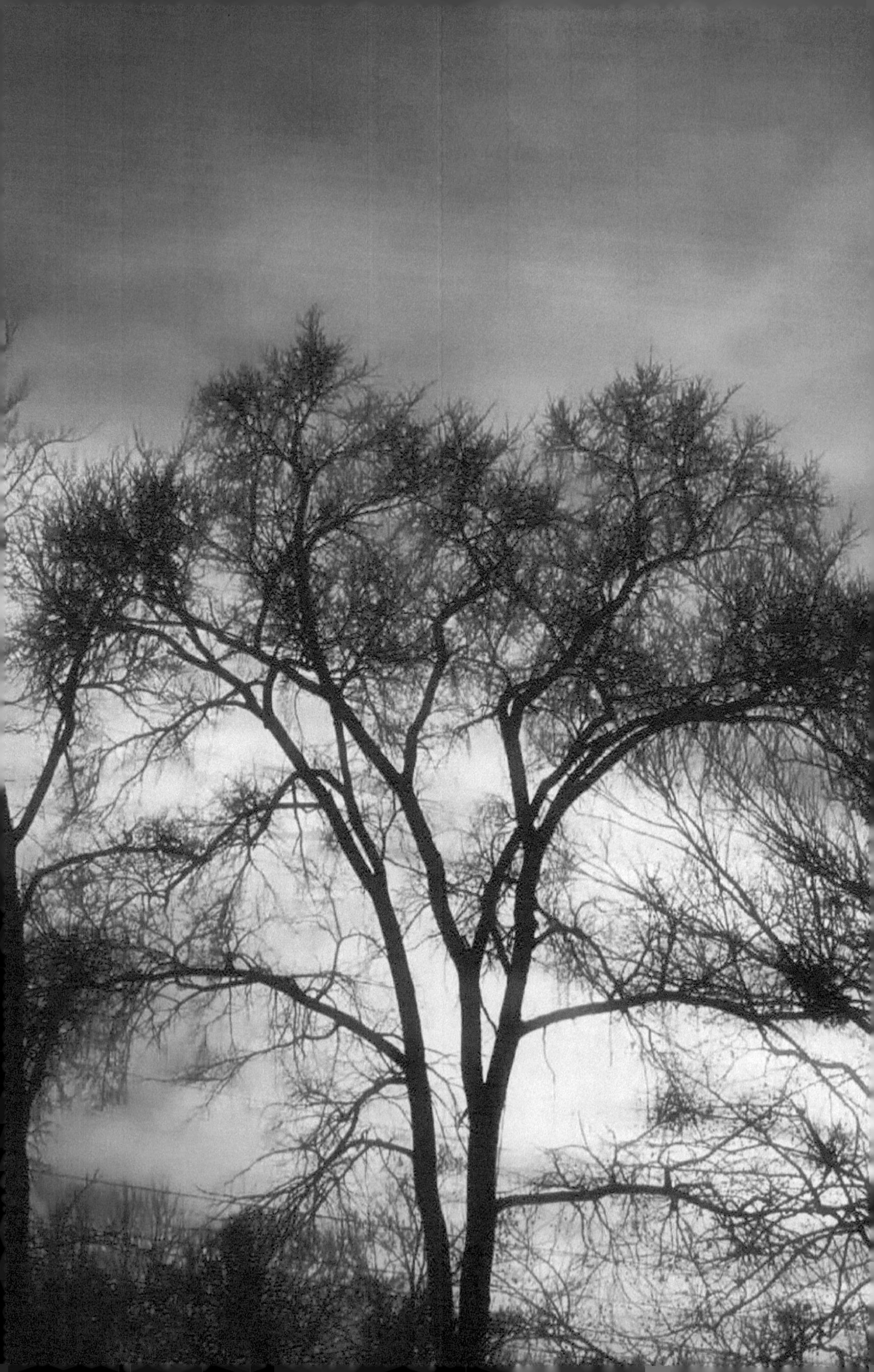

ALL CREATION

and she opened her arms
upon a cosmic wave she released the beats of an undying heart
the ancients answered, flooding the seas with souls
life eternal from the chalice we sipped
soaking upon her soil, where blooms fused with newborn breaths
to the call of the wild we danced, we wed
as the cedars praised and anointed us with eyes to see,
to be
to rise,
to fall
to sing,
to cry
to laugh,
to love
to whisper,
to scream
to learn,
to teach
to share,
to know
as she all the while sat in wait for us to return to her gates
feeding unto her the gifts we learned to share unto thee,
an allegiance of her love an undying rite
knowing passage comes not to all
that shan't sit beneath the shade hearing the trees
yet still giving, in hopes one day we'd all see
before the bell tolled.

Goddess
Jenny Hayut

As I sat upon a mountainside, with all the world before me
I observed the sun in the sky, running its daily course
And thought, *Isn't this the way things are supposed to be?*
The answer came to me easily, without doubt or remorse

All the world's money couldn't buy a bluer sky than this
Nothing could warm my heart more than sweet Wyoming sun
No worldly possession could ever bring more happiness
Than the satisfaction I feel here when every day is done

So if I ever leave this country
Its blue skies and western wind will always call me home
And I will stay on this road to follow wherever it goes
Some people may think that all I ever do is roam
But they don't know what I know—freedom is an open road

The other night, I heard wolves singing songs to the moon
And I thought I heard my name in their strange melodies
I hope I can hear their song again soon
Because to me, that song is as majestic as a symphony

When I smell these pines, I'm released from every stress
The rushing waters let me know I'm safe and sound
Without any help from man, the way nature planned is best
The bears and bison keep me company all around

So if I ever leave this country
Its blue skies and western wind will always call me home
And I will stay on this road to follow wherever it goes
Some people may think that all I ever do is roam
But they don't know what I know—freedom is an open road

Freedom is an Open Road
Robert Birkhofer

Water is erratic,
Unforgivingly so.
Currents swirl beneath,
A deceiving gentle flow.

Fire is fickle,
A flickering flame.
The desire and the passion;
A challenge to tame.

Air is dishonest,
Always inquisitive.
Playful with wind chimes,
An invisible fugitive.

The Earth is the source,
The roots and the soil.
Growth and production,
The labor and toil.

Battle of the Elements
Rachael Holmes

Sun woke me
hot-handed my shoulder
river already up, chattering
night too short
Jester in blue jumpsuit
begged off at dusk
to chase the comet
left me with bats in the belfry
rhyming up a tangle
until wee hours
Just when I nodded off
skunk came snuffling
for peanuts and blueberries
and other treasures
And the star-animals turned
on their dark carousel
cranking the night music

Night Music
Meredith Heller

Our Mother Matriarch
Her skin awash in panoramic tattoos
Ocean births new life with each wave
She surrenders to contractions of the moon

Her courage enduring suffering and decay
Her dead children fueling new life
Scars and blemishes tell of motherhood
For life and death she is pastor and midwife

She bends in strength to our machines
Through sacrifice still meeting every need
For a humble knee protects more than the unbent
But even she cannot satisfy our greed

And yet we speak lies of her daily
"private property" signs objectify her through
Her assets renamed as resources
How can you own Her that made you?

Matriarch
Hidden Bear

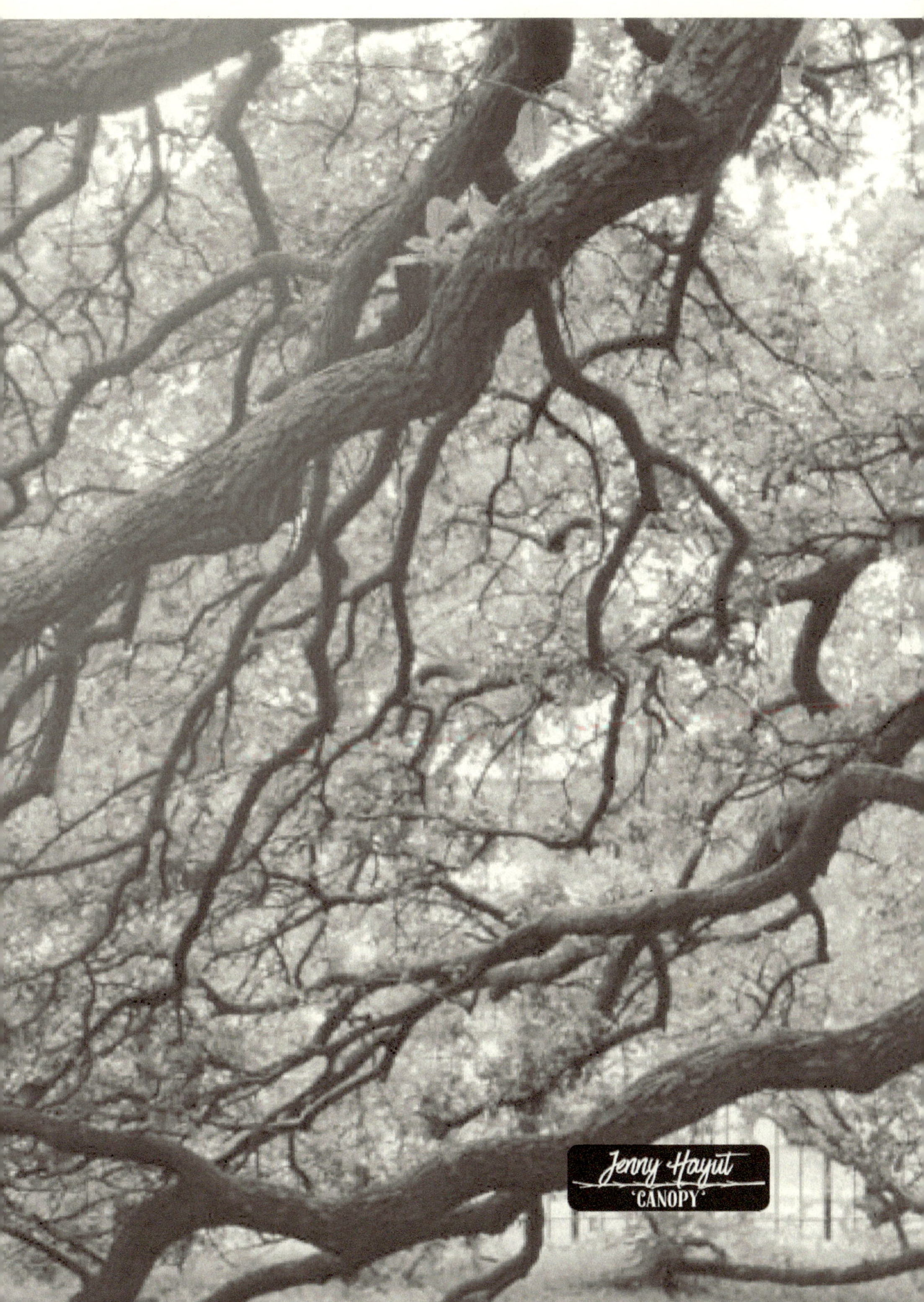
Jenny Hayut
'CANOPY'

Don't they stop time
stop the spinning
stop the world
like a soft landing
commands attention
As if gravity had been given
Some new agenda

Don't they make us lean,
tilt to every word~
What are they saying?
What do they sing?
All at once, all of them
whisper, they say

the quiet is waiting
your stillness lets listen
where the world will come
to lie at your feet.
there you can hear
what we have been saying
in each of your
three hundred
thousand
years.

What the Leaves Whisper
R.H. Alexander

she is scooped up by the abrasive desert wind
the forced settlement cannot break her spirit
in her arid bed sleeps her shallow roots

she is thirsty for life
the desert rain is often light and brief
too sudden and too short lived for most
for her,
she thrives in conditions others wither

she despises mediocre
the desert sun is scorching and wearing
long suffering brings out her vibrancy
nature trials her with extreme heat and cold
she births uplifting pigments to protect her fragile pose

she is beaten by the violent sandstorm
leaf scorched, foliage torn, uprooted
it seems that she has nothing left to fight
until she senses the coming of fog
and tastes the sweetness of dew

Desert Succulents
Cassa Bassa

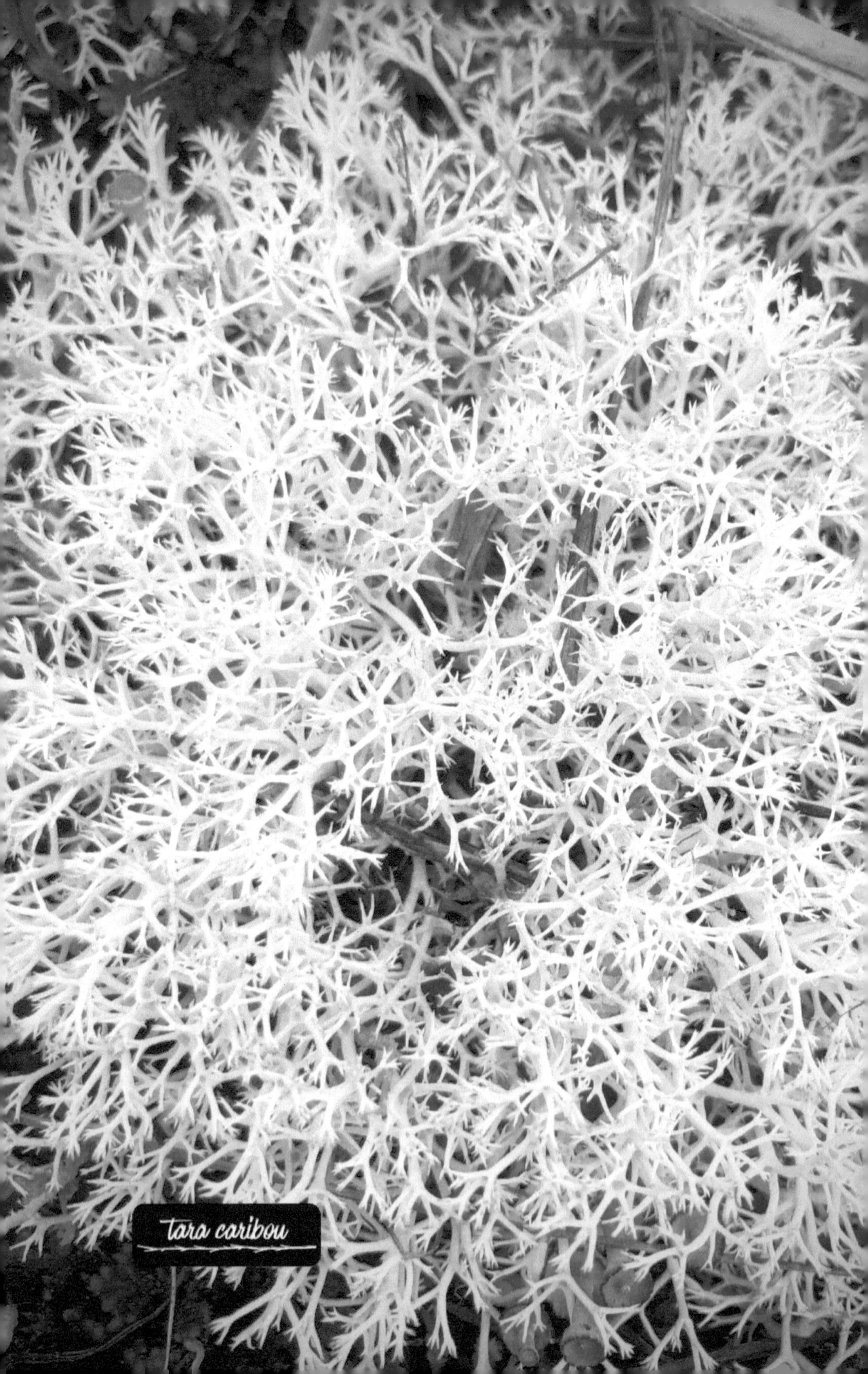
tara caribou

Today, as I often do,
I surrendered
to the music of the ocean waves
surging and retreating
against the shore,
the birds,
oh the birds!
in their marvelous song,
chirps and whistles and shrill remarks,
the fuzzy bumblebees
and the flies and hornets
buzzing suddenly as they move
from dandelion to dandelion,
water cascading over the cliffs' edge
flowing in drops and rivulets,
as only water can,
sandhill cranes bugle
to their lovers and kin,
a distant dog yips and barks.
They all create a monstrous symphony
each and every day...
we only have to listen.

A Natural Symphony
tara caribou

Heartbeat thundering in my chest
The trail wraps through forests time forgot
I gaze up through the canopy
underbrush plagues me and I lose my thought

The map abandoned I rush onward
Headfirst into unbroken landscape
I feel a roar burst from my chest
Birds shuttering in my wake

Galloping; a wild horse in the wind
Gliding down hills and through rivers
Overtaken by my lust for the forest
Running until the sunsets light slivers

Resting at last amidst a natural world
Night sounds harmonize a symphony
I rest my head on moss laden terrain
I feel the wild space infect me, willingly.

Trail Run
Hidden Bear

Remember to dream like coyotes
Howling under coruscating skies
Blot out the din and the bullshit
Sketch in the vast constellations
As you lie back into warm sand
Bare your blood dripping fangs
And smile like a mad cracked beast
Like love-struck mosquitoes
Proselytize your ecstasy
Of rivers and wilderness
Seek that which is buried
Above the pine kissed air
Arise from concrete pabulum
Dust off your umbilical cord
Rip it from the thumbs of awkward apes
Discover how your body moves
When dancing on the brink of death
Pour a beer over the maws
Of grizzly and storm and rock
Be proud to look them in the eye
And once you are safely back
You will be unable to provide any
answer to "how was the trail?"
just growl and circle in your cage
restless, skinny, and ready to run.

Animal
Cara Feral

If you look from a certain
corner of your eye
you may see the moon-faced
Buddhas
who live in the rocks
who throw you a twinkle
and a kiss
before retreating
to their hovel
where the counsel
has commenced
If you tilt your ear
to the space between
the notes
of the rapids
you may hear the Selkies
singing
in the serpentine
Clean is the granite
that reflects the sun
on the palms
of the planet
as we orbit
the summit
of its burning face
Wind churns the water
traces her fingers
at the border
where the gloaming
approaches with grace

Gloaming
Meredith Heller

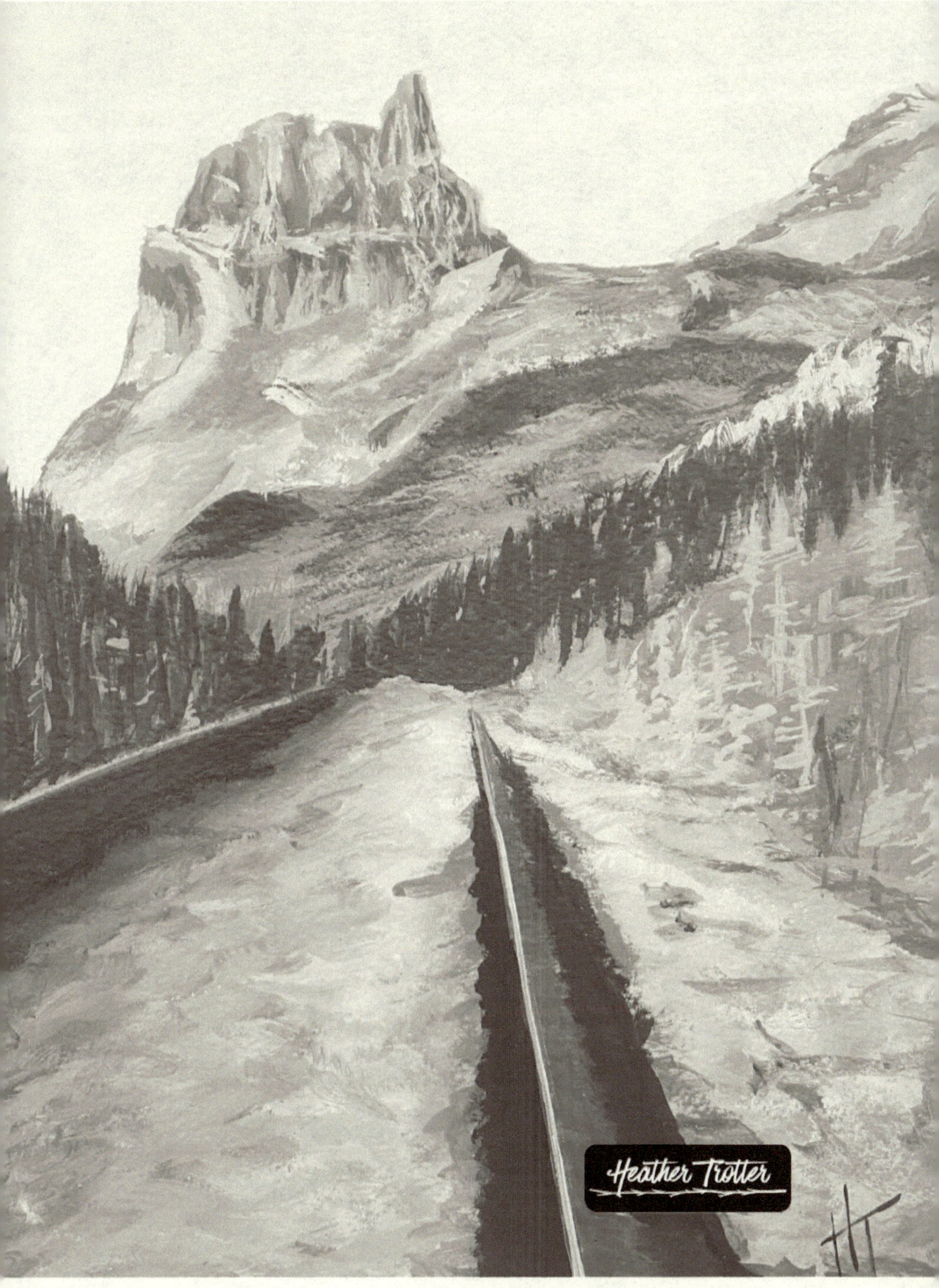

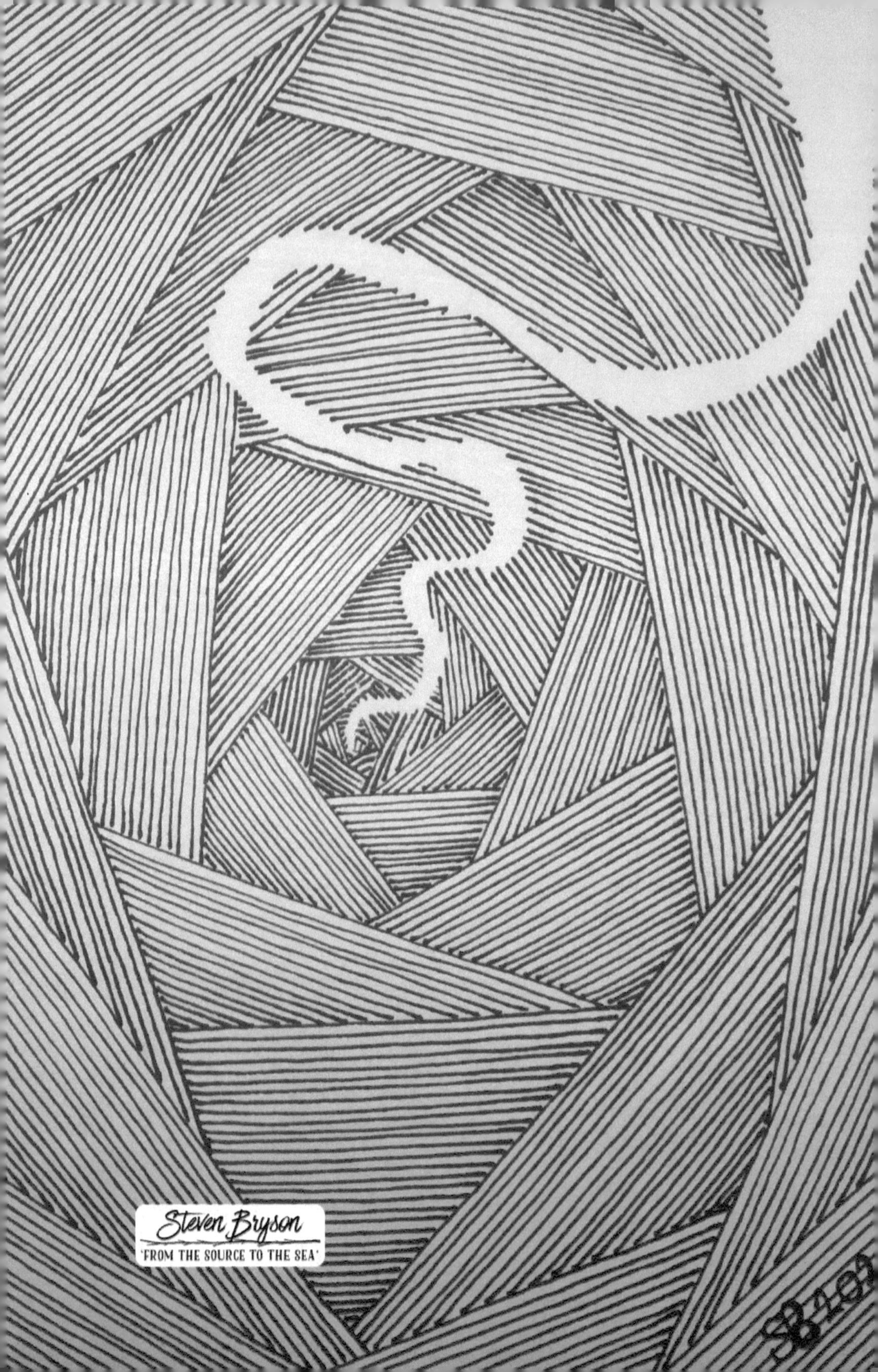
Steven Bryson
'FROM THE SOURCE TO THE SEA'

An island unto thyself.
In a sea that swims and breaks with waves of discontent.
You raise the flag on the mound.
That sword, you bring on down to me.
Yet I build a world around you.
Like a town on a volcano.
Climbing higher for a better view.
Yet a rumbling in the belly of the beast is heard.
Daily, I wait for black rain.
But hope for the sun to shine.
Yet the rumble can be assuaged.
As I climb to the lip and taste the lava.
Kissing your plume of red and dangerous fire.
On high, I can see the turrets of other kingdoms.
Their flags, bound and bright in the tropical sun.
Happy under the banner of the one.
Yet I remain, rooted to the hard cooled magma that is your soul.
Knowing the end, will have me buried like the people of Pompeii.
Frozen in time, in ecstatic pain and awe.

Volcano
Mark Ryan

A night-bird shrieks, a hyena cackles
Orion strides the sky in his belt of she-tortoises
while shooting stars carve graceful arcs
over the dark and silent veld

Trance-like they stare into red-ochre flames
tiniest specks in a timeless universe
each one smaller than a newly-hatched mantis
gathered in this place of the ancient ones

They feed the fire, cast another spell of herbs
sparks crackle in the desiccated air
Herb-scented smoke hangs purple in the dusk
ochre and red stained faces, mesmerized, begin

Deep throat humming, sound ever-swelling
Standing, stomping, the ancient dance begins
Hands clap, ankle-shells rattle
staccato vibrations crash around the rocks

Thunder booms, the rain-bull bellows
blankets of rain sweep to greet the distant sea
And in the morning, the long-legged rain-cow
will bring soft rain to last the season.

The Summoning
Chris Hall

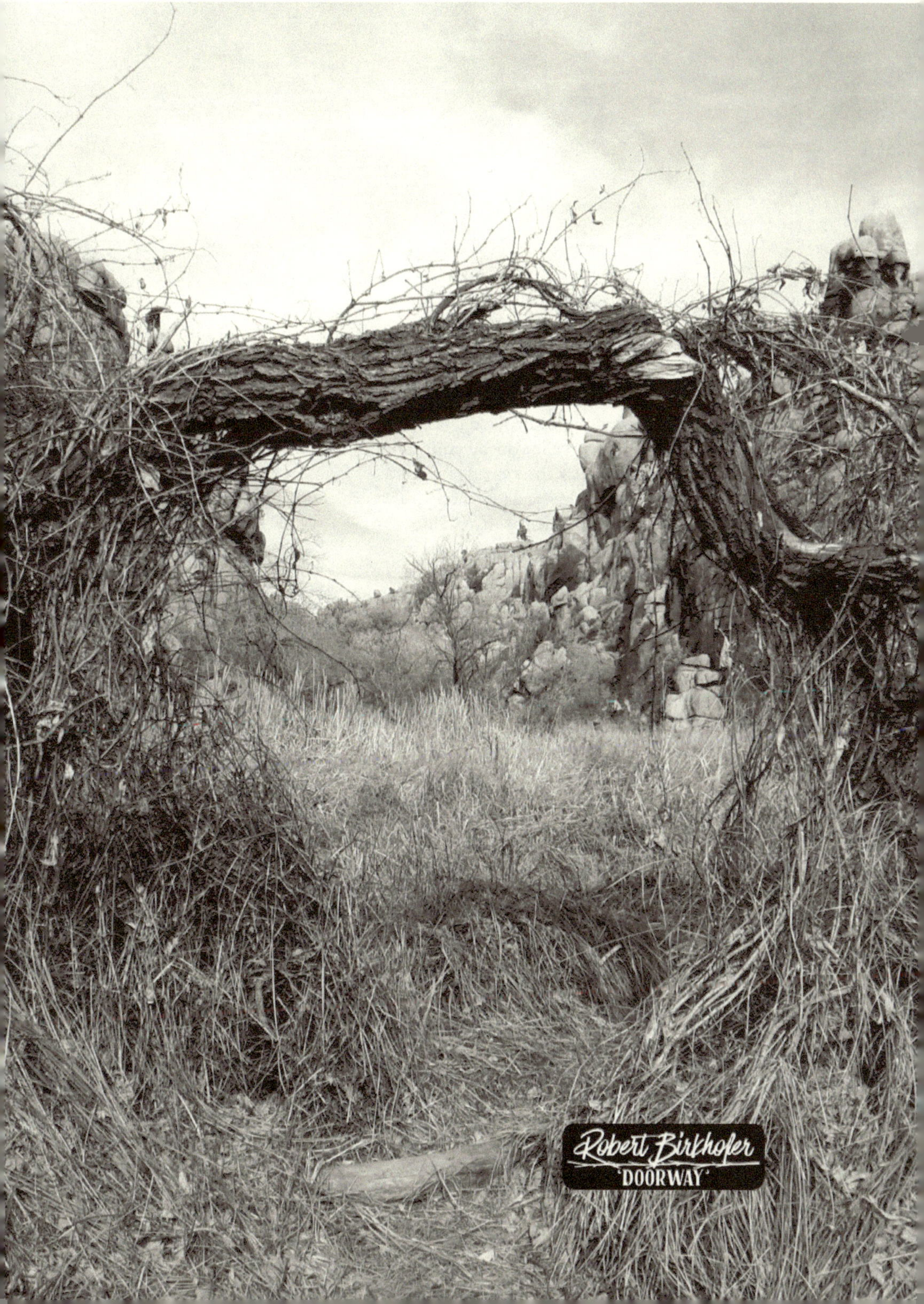
Robert Birkhofer
'DOORWAY'

I came to give you flowers
sealed with parched lips
I hope they survive the journey
through the many galaxies

The ground in which you lay
is the only place left
that calls you by your name
I read the carvings made
on the heavy crown you wear
as I wait for my calling
to see you once again

"I have stripped down all my masks
to embark on a distant adventure
to walk amongst the stars
to fly amidst the clouds
and wait at Heaven's gate
with you to reunite"

Tombstone
Donna Nongkhlaw

I fell in love with Mother Nature's sunset
In awe of the sterling rays of the moonlight
Enchanted with the hope of the rainbow
Radiance was born in the brittle clouds
To cleanse in the lake of meditation is bliss
Soothing wind whispers in the morning

I applaud the brisk rain on mountains
Serenity blooms like a sunflower
Purity sprinkles joy on the soft ground
I cherish the kiss of the daylight
Shadows creeping on the discovered truth
A simple interpretation and point of view

I embrace the weeping sounds of the night
Familiarity seeping in my hands with a brush stroke
Saturated with every color of the seasons
A logical but endearing artist from the inside
Sensitivity dripping and scars engraved
Yet love spills in the beauty of the canvas

Painting the essence from Rosebud Café

Painting from Rosebud Café
Braeden Michaels

warm skin,
and blue sky speckled
with delicate dogwood;
earth erupting with
tulips the size of hope.

my favorite season feels like
absence this year--
like nature chose
the wrong metaphor.

"read the room,"
I think; and then

"maybe it's the thought that counts?"

I walk unmoved
by this beauty--
dragging heavy limbs
fueled by a vague
and withering notion
that "this is good for me."

increasingly unconvinced
with lack of any tangible evidence, but here we are.

strolling this picture perfect day
feeling flat and joyless;
I take pictures, for later--
when maybe my beauty-loving
heart will be revived.

in spite of myself,
something subtle in me stirs:

my God, but did you see
how that pink tree sets
the sky on fire?

Beautiful Apocalypse
fara tucker

winter is mind numbingly long
staring at the icicles

they dove down like pool splash
from the overwhelmed roof
formed a curtain to
shield my tiresome eyes
from the morning haze

sometimes they look like
a baby's temper tantrum tears

sometimes they glare at me like
a group of flying darts

sometimes they bloom like
frozen dandelions

winter is mind numbingly long

today they resemble
my hair turned grey overnight
I should have kept
hibernating

Icicles
Cassa Bassa

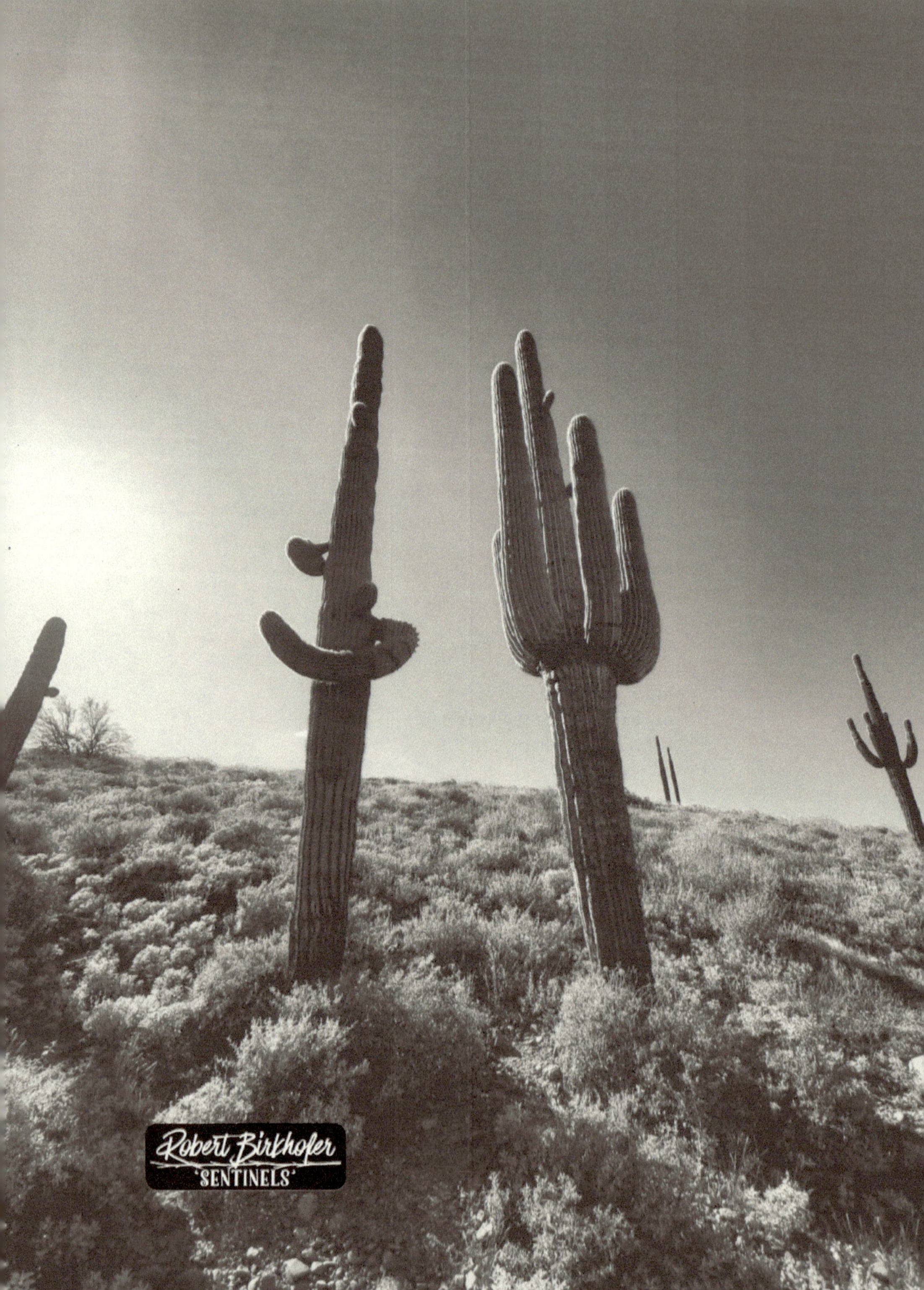
Robert Birkhofer
'SENTINELS'

There is no romance in this land
Just tiny elf owlets begging in desperate chorus
From their hollowed saguaro
For their mother's catch
And the ferocious beating of insect wings
Against the searing air like the dying gasp
Of an old plodding bass drum
Everything is poisonous or stings or pricks or bites
Behind the chaparral bush and rare cacti bloom
The coiled rattler's warning thrum
With the soul of a poet and
The soles of a dead man hiking
I'll walk 700 miles through this place
Just to hold her hand
Out here it's not what we acquire
But how shit gets moved around

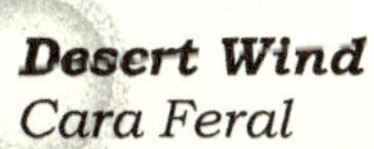

Desert Wind
Cara Feral

in the distance a voice thunders
irate, inconsolable
a thousand stones raining down
high to low, gaining momentum

a mother bear with suckling cubs
cowers in her den
a hare, its ears flat against its back,
lays motionless in the thicket
but for the twitch of its nose

even the raven, with her blue-black feathers
closes her beak, twists her head,
tilting and pitching her neck
ever so slightly
to catch a better glimpse,
takes wing silently

from the cold blue she sees him there
shaking, tormented, alone in his ire
the raven tips her wing
angles back around
then tucks her wings for speed
and continues west
without a backwards glance

in his agony and bitterness,
he notices her not,
instead shouts and bellows his anger,
his sadness, his utter despair
until in a fit of rage, unprovoked
he vomits his fiery mania,
a passion of violence

birds burst from their branches,
the sow, two cubs in tow,
barrels down the shale gravel slope
the hare and the deer and the pine marten
the fox and the wolverine forgo their animosity
in a moment of terror,
abandon their burrows for lower ground

his unjust revulsion continues
belching and blowing and
spewing from his mouth until,
with a final shudder,
he is, for a moment, at peace

he grumbles,
turns then falls into a fitful sleep,
at times shifting or restive but
his fury, for now, lies dormant
until the next time he awakens

Unprovoked Enmity
tara caribou

Drink deep the color wheel of sunrise
Let waterfall mist cover your face
The smell of pine needles overwhelm
With the songbird rhythm echo in space

Let river rapids play white noise
Shadows shelter you overhead
Rest on this ancient boulder now
Even as the sunsets in amber red

Let fire warm you through night
Rewilding and finding nature's home
Bathe in the moonlit air
Soul longing once again to roam

Mentor
Hidden Bear

I hear the mountains calling to my soul
As clear as if they called me by my name
The shore-bound waves upon the lake do roll
Reflecting peaks majestic and unchanged
The heights where few, save eagles, dare to roam
I lift my eyes and set my feet to go

Now, gentle waters flow across the trail
And soft pine leaves emit their fragrant bliss
Life's worries wilt, becoming rather frail
Compared with peace as absolute as this
I tread along the path that is sublime
Of those who wander wild amongst the pines

A single flower blooms on forest floor
The color of the innocence of spring
As delicate as clouds above that soar
Arrayed in greater splendor than a king
Rich tapestries, painted with oils divine
Surround and awe this humbled heart of mine

I sit here in the quiet, thinking long
On life, on love, on solitude and joy
Upon my ears, there rests a tuneful song
The sighing wind, by mighty peaks giv'n voice
It whispers secrets kept within the minds
Of those who wander wild amongst the pines

Moist fog covers me in a soft blanket
A mystic shroud that hides the land below
The path ahead beckons—I must take it
New worlds emerge as higher up I go
Atop the peaks: freedom unthinkable
Above the clouds: beauty unspeakable

Mud on these boots of mine bears testament
To where I've walked—tomorrow, new paths wait
When one adventure ends, do not lament
All trails connect—it's what the wise ones say
I count it good fortune to walk in line
With those who wander wild amongst the pines

Those Who Wander Wild
Robert Birkhofer

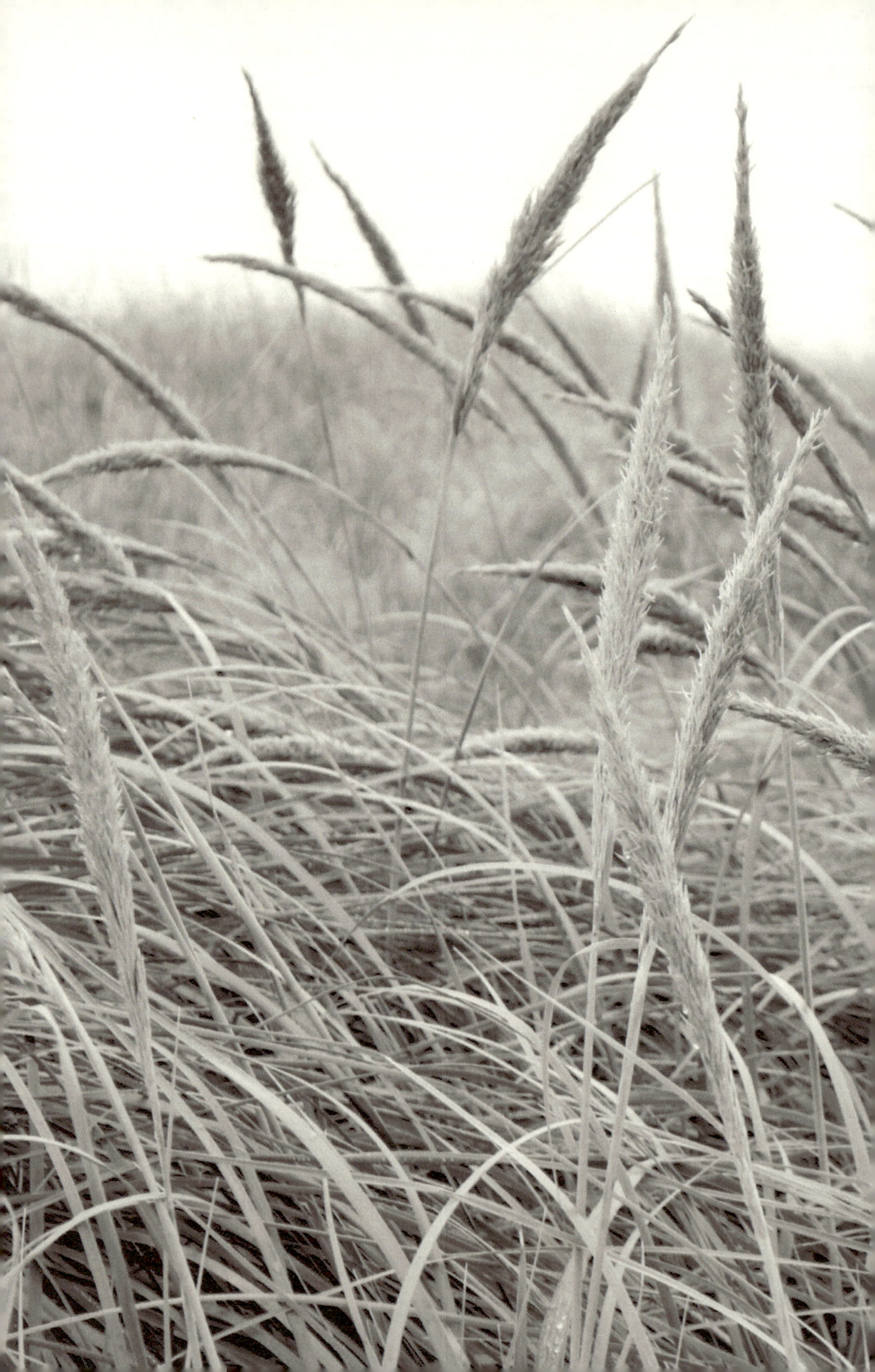

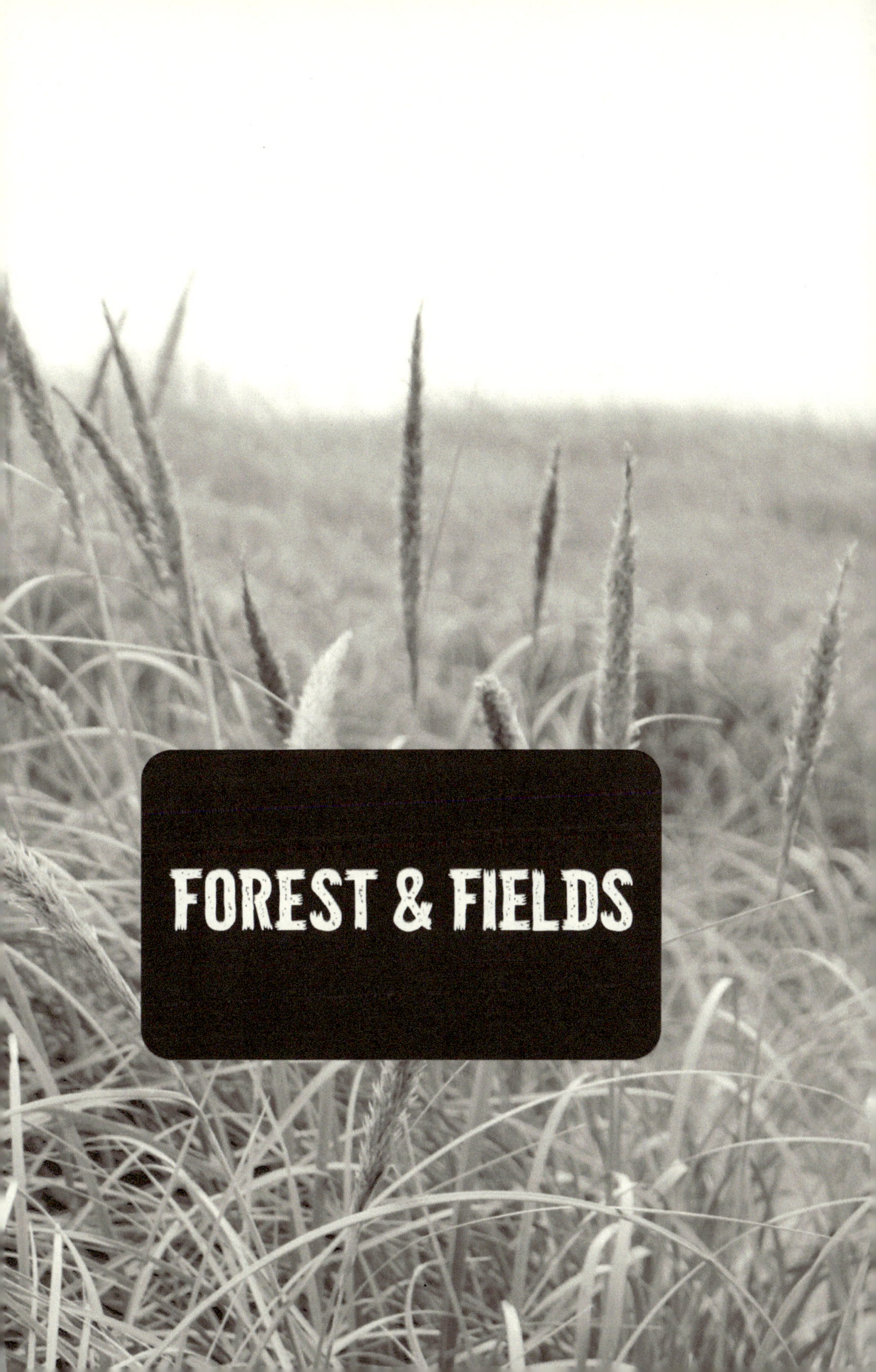
FOREST & FIELDS

Flowers grow in disorganized patches,
Scattered clusters to match my muddled mind.
My dormant, creative heart unlatches,
A rainbow revived with colors combined.

I walk among the magenta pansies,
Remembering times of laughter, void of,
Misplaced joy and contentment, within these
Memories, of a lonesome turtle dove.

These loving thoughts ignite my heart, a-glow.
I rediscover warmth, long forgotten,
In every buttery shade of yellow.
Finding solace in blooms of white cotton.

I collect snow-white pansies, as above,
As souvenirs of resurrected love.

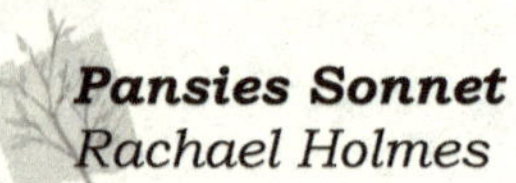

Pansies Sonnet
Rachael Holmes

I ran naked through the oaks
crunching freshly fallen leaves
I made it to the treeline's edge
as I tried to catch the breeze

I stopped to catch my breath
when I reached the open plains
Whereby tall grass I was greeted
and I noticed something strange

I heard the full moon call
A faint whisper it was at first
Imploring me to recharge
and keep warm under her light's surge

I lay down upon the valley
cradled in her glow
For once I felt at peace
and I knew I was finally home

When the Full Moon Calls
Stephanie Lamb

Your hawthorn coat
Hung heavy with the kiss of Spring,
The scent of rebirth,
Its heady fragrance seeping into my pores
With the touch of the new
The delicacy of the past,
Creeping upon me like a familiar curse,
Beneath the field maple and the oak
Whose wisdom reaches out from the edges to the depths
Whispers across the glades and brooks -
'Come to me now',
Withered arm branches
Ill-prepared for the weight of the new,
The expected that arrives too soon,
But brings the light to life,
Wrap themselves around the spaces
That grow between our hearts
Turn the barren to green
And swell with the pride of parenthood
As our tentative footsteps
Brush the forest floor.

The Wisdom of the Oak
Chris Nelson

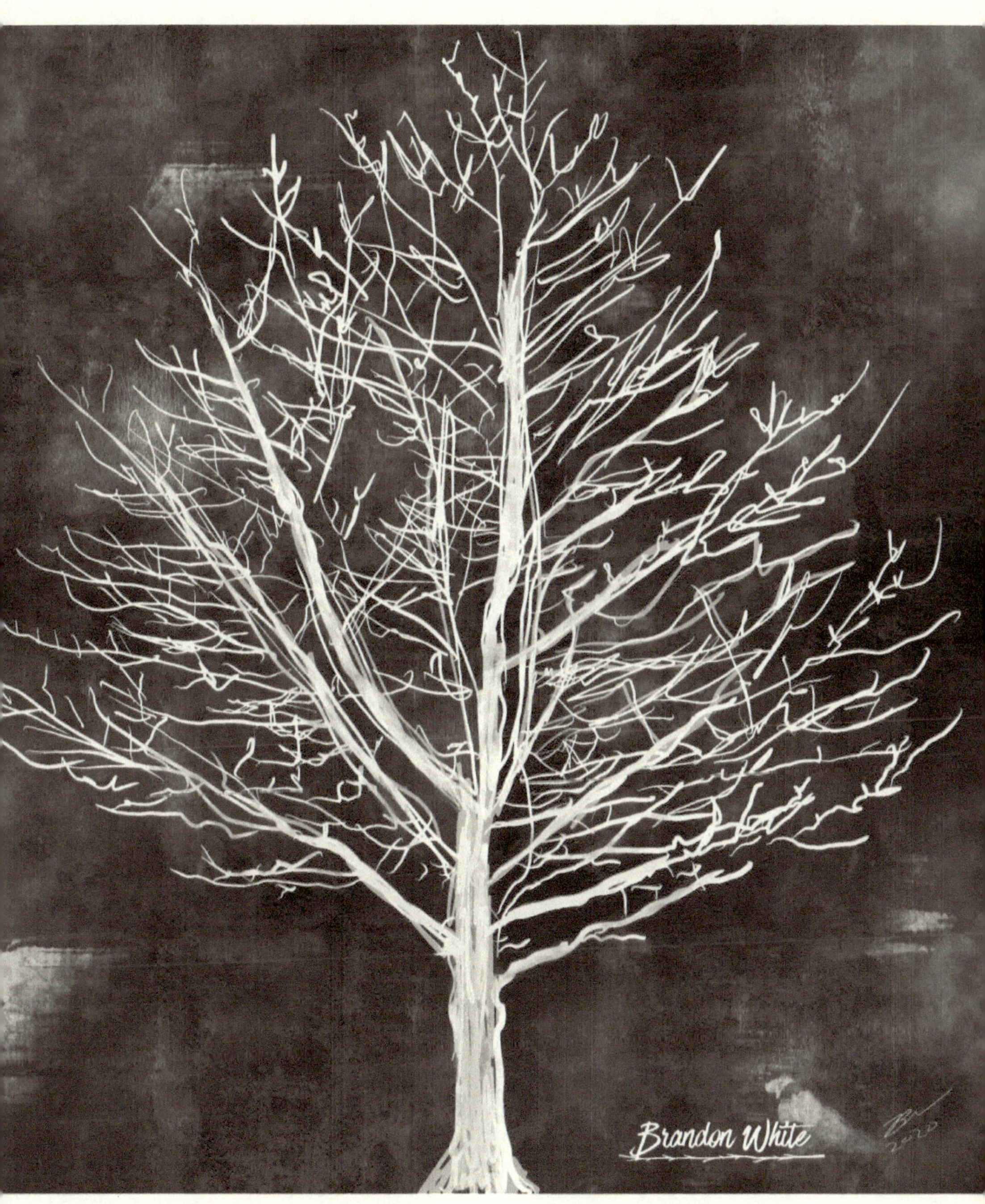
Brandon White

I own nothing of you
nor this leaf that shivers
into a half-bud above
the phlox and blue flax
that burrow with me
into this old winter grass.
Yet how much I yearn
for your blue-struck wing
like an arrow over a sun
struck river, as if it were some
prayer to fit between
my strange and lonely palm,
so hollow its feathers,
so frail I could breathe through them,
so iridescent the sky
you harbor down that
whoever hammered this wood
together did so
in such hurry, in such
love, that even the nails
were left unflattened. And now
your nestling waits
at this world someone
cored into the box for it
to see: a little
knot of light,
a song
to dip and break against.

To the Swallow This Spring
at the Nest Box
Kathryn Winograd

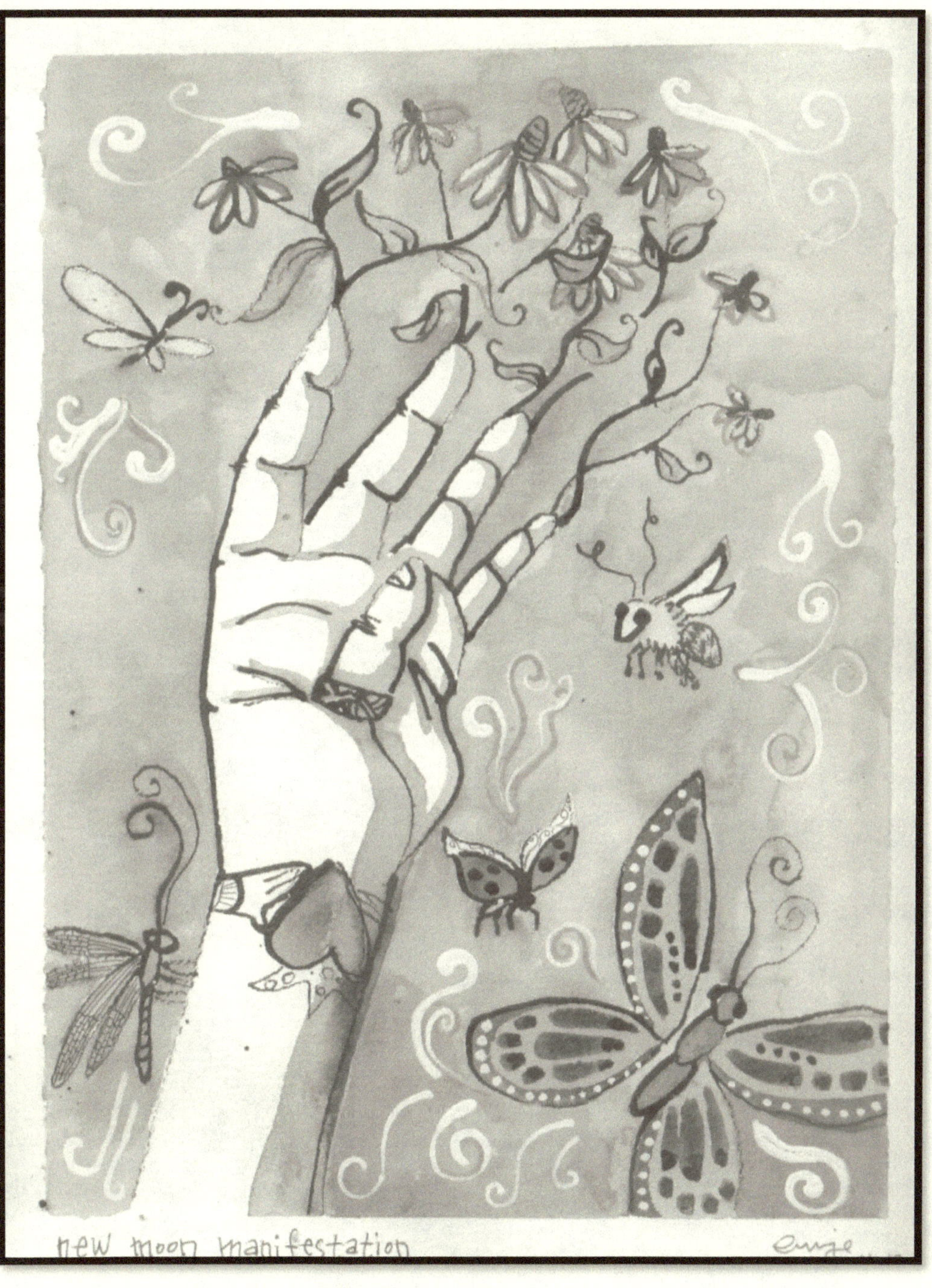
new moon manifestation

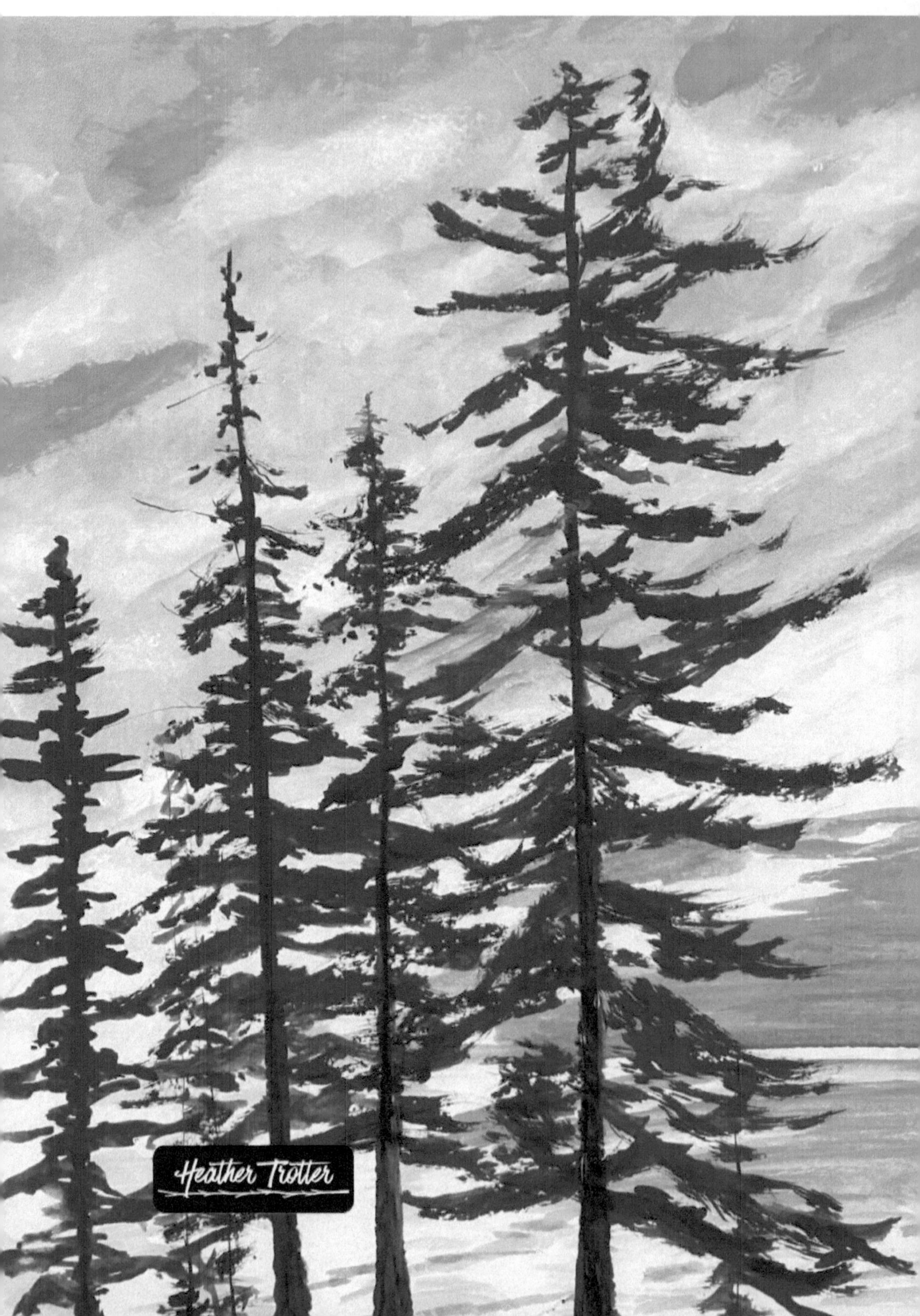
Heather Trotter

Needle pines in palms.
The leaves grow, flow and blossom off these fingertips.
The brush of the wind, like the breath of mother earth, rustles what has formed.
Green, like the emerald forests that now hold my bones.
They sway and swoon, catching the dying sun.
Holding onto the little jewels of oxygen for a moment too long.
Before the great exhale.
A chance to turn clouds into mountains that sail over tempting shores.
The leaves, bitter smelling like eucalyptus and amphetamines.
Fragrant and fragile, that break at a careless touch.
For the sun often harms, and this brittle heart demands a different type of love.
Shaded and soft, like a kiss from butterfly feet.
Touching these olive blades deep.
High, tall and commanding if left in the sight of love.
These leaves, fronds of sweet depth cruise upwards.
Wanting to touch the sky.

Verdure Adjustment
Mark Ryan

Beyond the forest floor,
blankets of needles and rot,
you sit, a king on thrones
of wriggling legs, moistened dew.

Red, you bleed color
onto acres bleak and grey,
tainted brown by fallen limbs,
dusty rocks, dehydrated petals.

Will you stay this way
as winter's blusters arrive?
Crimson amongst the soil,
solid and crisp on dampened earth?

Your forest, a monument
to empty days of Autumn
soaked, drenched in your colors
soon to coagulate to softened green

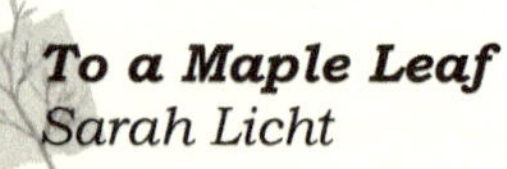

To a Maple Leaf
Sarah Licht

They come soundless as if afloat
the little animals assemble
to watch, to be reminded this is more
than a tiny shrug from the world
They are here to learn
What they learn keeps them alive

The snarl of a coyote in a bear's jaws
the muffle of the snap of its bones
A raccoon's shriek, eaten alive by a wolf
How it all ends cut clean, the way a razor
singes the night air with its arc.
Death stops near, shrugs, moves on

When the deer starts to wobble
the assembled lower their heads,
fidgety boys in church. They circle
as if biting their tail will make them immune
They jigger knees helplessly.

His legs fold under, the antlers get heavy and tilt.
One beam touches the ground for the first time
lifts then touches again, testing the earth's hold
under all this weight. Eyes fade and glaze but never close
long after this work is done.

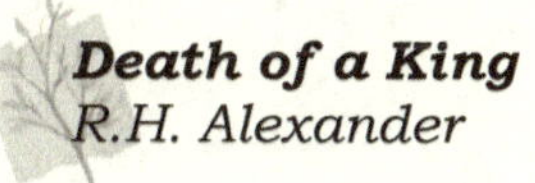

Death of a King
R.H. Alexander

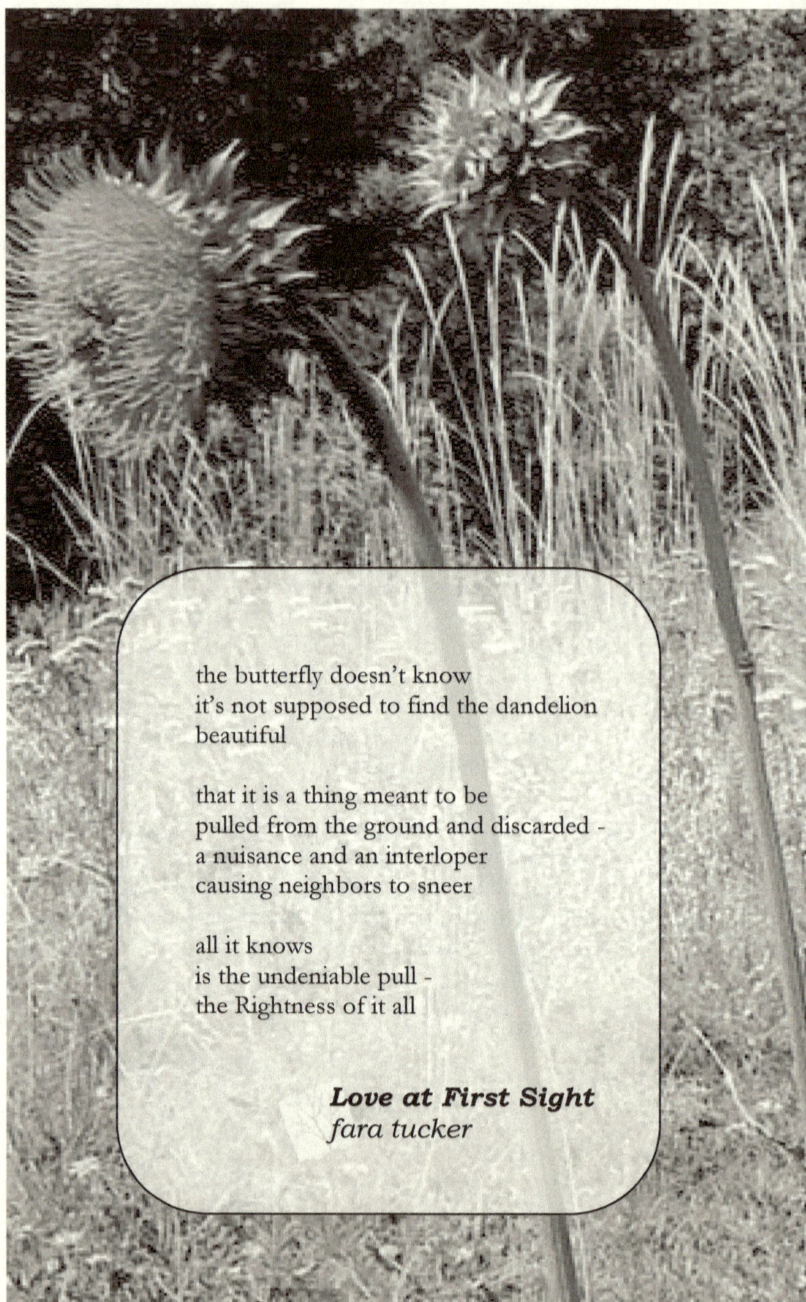

the butterfly doesn't know
it's not supposed to find the dandelion
beautiful

that it is a thing meant to be
pulled from the ground and discarded -
a nuisance and an interloper
causing neighbors to sneer

all it knows
is the undeniable pull -
the Rightness of it all

Love at First Sight
fara tucker

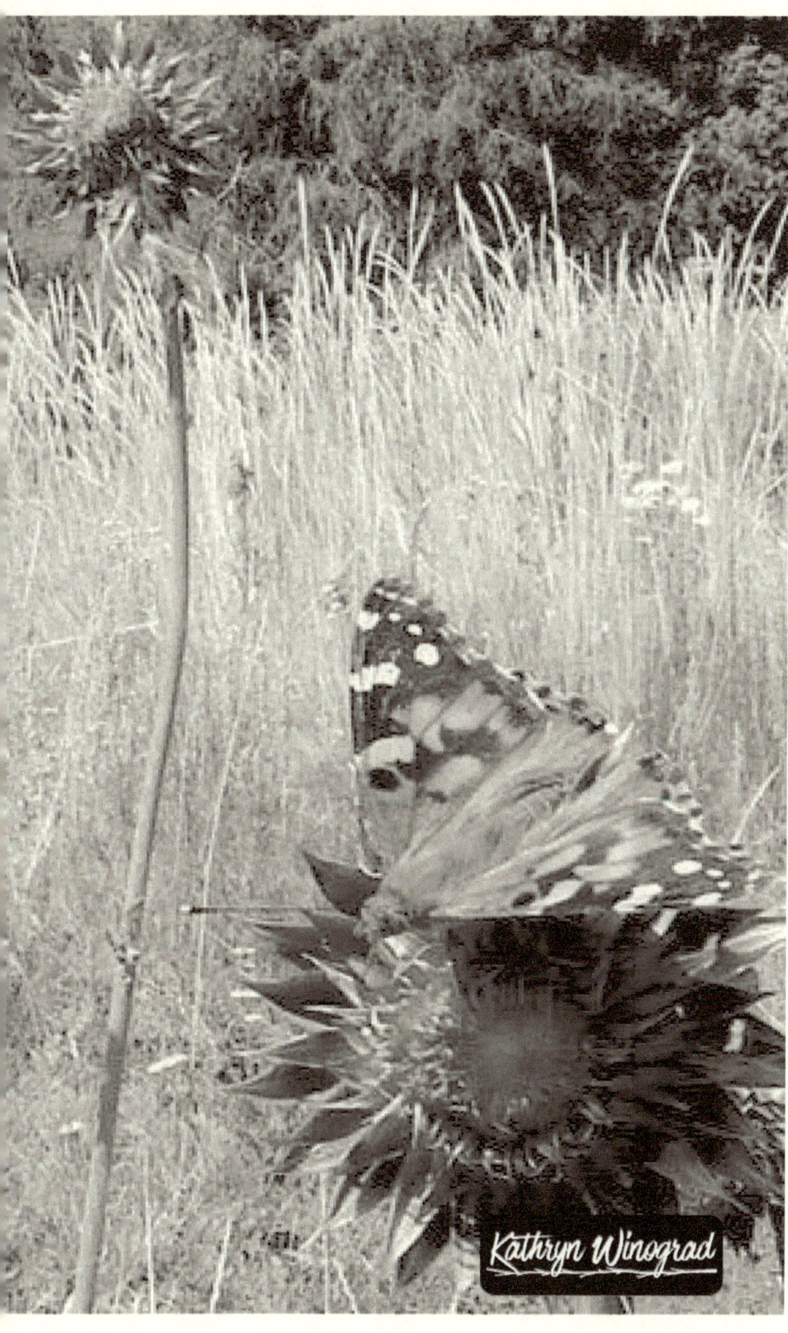
Kathryn Winograd

Camouflage of colors,
Bark of brown shades,
Boneless of black and grey rocks,
Mosses of light green and black patches,
Silent roars of reddish orange colored forest,
Bleak of dry antelope of the yellow deer,
Reflection of rainbow,
Upon the purple murky river,
The fierce alligator prowls in blue,
The fierce tiger roams in dark,
The tones of color,
Combines the spectrum of emotion,
Just like the habitat in the forest.

Nature Color
Jainisha Sadacharam

Sunflowers seem to sprout
from the sands,
as if a nurturing sun god
makes them rise and bloom
without question

My mind has flowers, too
taking root, one by one
I touch their gentle petals,
feel their elongated stems,
trying to understand
what my thoughts signify
and where my words flow

Hoping my flowering thoughts
are as eloquent as Emerson or Frost
that suddenly appear
from my lips
as I speak.

Sunflowers In The Sand
Mark Tulin

canopies of moss
coat the heirlooms of blooms
as knowing petals, much wiser than she
wander upon the forest of green
unhurried steps kiss the soil
as earthen creatures awaken
to follow her through the seeds of time
she sips the wind, a wise friend to the shade
for the lust of the sun is but a myth here
a singsong to her soul, she bows to the call
as narcissus blades and violas dance upon the river's edge
burying her head into springtime's perfume
the minnows peek and birds rest their wings
to catch a glimpse of she,
their Persephone

Maiden of the Shades
Jenny Hayut

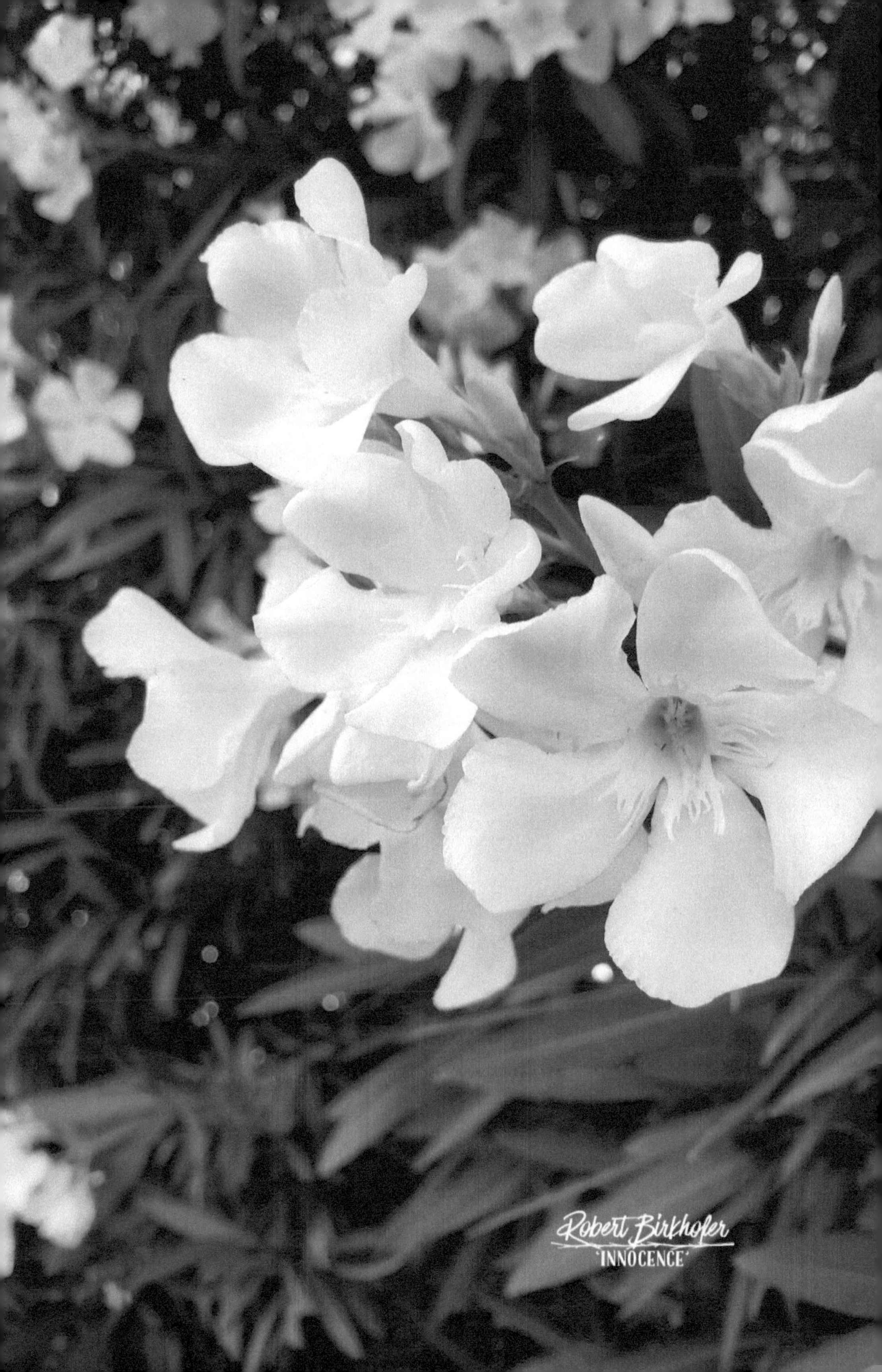
Robert Birkhofer
'INNOCENCE'

He prayed to God
for spring to come
So she would
arise.

Instead a serpent
Flicked its tongue,
And whispered him
A lie.

For when it came
It came with frost;
Glistening dew drops
softly caught
In spiral leaves,
Quickening
to icy oracles
on her spine.

I would have waited
passionately,
To someday call
Her mine.

Rather than pray
"sooner"
He should have prayed
"alive."

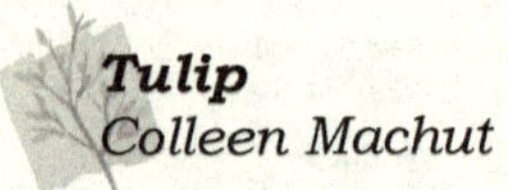

Tulip
Colleen Machut

The sapling took stock of others
Clamoring for impossible heights
Hungry and driven to placate
The sapling sought out light

Up was the traditional direction
Leaves and branches eclipsing
But the canopy was fulfilled
Was a new direction worth risking?

The wind blew incomparable
Angling the sapling parallel the earth
Roots dug deep and they choose
Outward to find the lights worth

Years of mocking at new direction
But a decade and the others had withered
The saplings leaves graced by warm glow
Patience, belief and new direction delivered

Seeking Sapling
Hidden Bear

The humming bird mistakes
me for a flower: something
half-wan and camouflaged
in a wild iris shirt.
The bare aspens riddle
the sun's slant like snakes
of shade. Far off,
past the pines, a meadow
lark trills from the spring.
Yesterday, I found
bear scat fresh,
flies swarming it,
so I walked, clapping
my hands until they hurt.
The air stirs.
The hummingbird
zips past the porch,
circles, hovers, a tiny
god at my face.
I am all blossom
and sepal, sweet petals
and wing dust.
And at my feet, a tiny bee
crawls for the first time.

Morning on a Cabin Porch
Kathryn Winograd

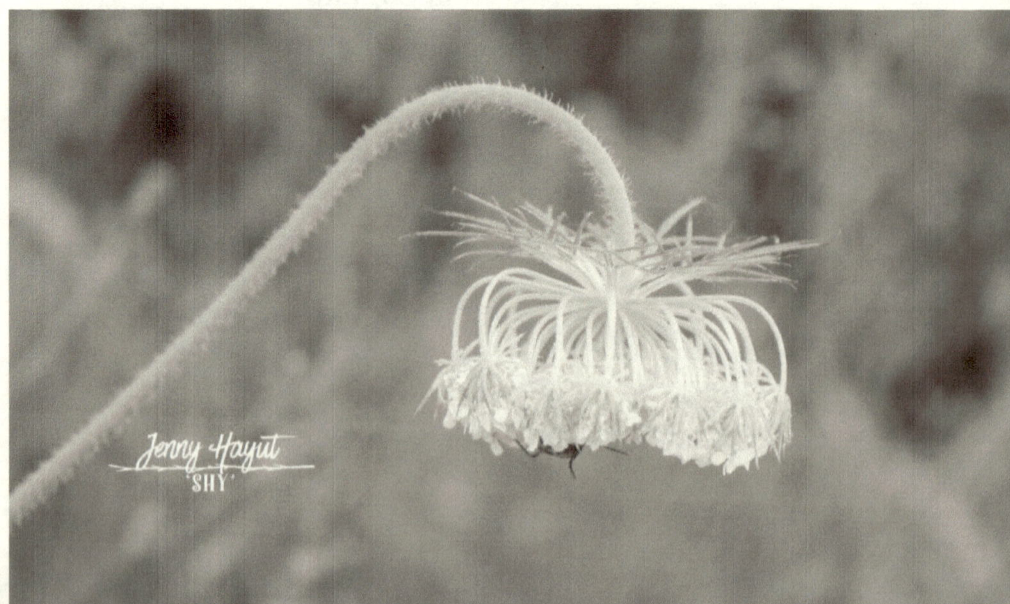

Swept down from the hills
Carried by the weight of expectation
Which hung like a millstone medallion
Snaking silent a serpent searching
Fulfillment's promise
Goal-driven by the endless sea
Whose arms open and close
Like a feasting mouth
Ever hungry for the taste of the new
As ragged rocks mount themselves
An army standing firm
Against the raging course of time
The swells and currents which tire
Yet relentless rise and fall
And now with the safety of shadows
Cast and lost
A distant memory
Whose source slips hidden
Far from slight
The flatlands call out
Their plaintive cry
As turns straighten purpose-lost
And passion fades beneath
A lengthening Sun
Swallowed by the voracious fens
Which run towards the shore
To drive the sea away.

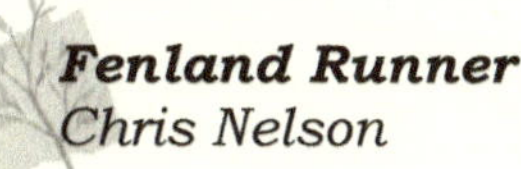

Fenland Runner
Chris Nelson

The breeze-caressed veld sways
sending dry waves to break on a distant shore
whirlwind dust-devils dance over bare earth
rising up to be scorched into stillness.

Evening swells across the veld
and the thorn tree's shadow
reaches out with tendril fingers
to caress the smudge-blue foothills.

As daylight fades, the breeze quickens
and the new maiden emerges
standing on the threshold of the distant koppie
in that powerful place between hearth and wilderness.

She turns and kneels at the young man's side
offering herself to him.
Limbs entwine and under the eyes of the ancestors
they become one.

Darkness closes in and the great African she-moon rises
pin-prick stars stab the violet-thick night
and now the once-maiden cries out
her triumphant ululation echoing across the empty veld.

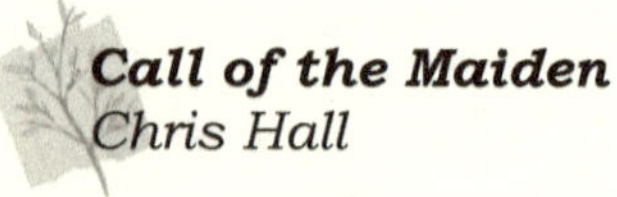

Call of the Maiden
Chris Hall

Whitetails learn to explode
when traction is the thinnest node
between life and next

One slip and fangs close in
weapons once, now tools, begin
their chuff and hum in red snow

The End of Things stops by to nod
without judgment on lesser gods
then keeps its pace and moves along.

In Red Snow
R.H. Alexander

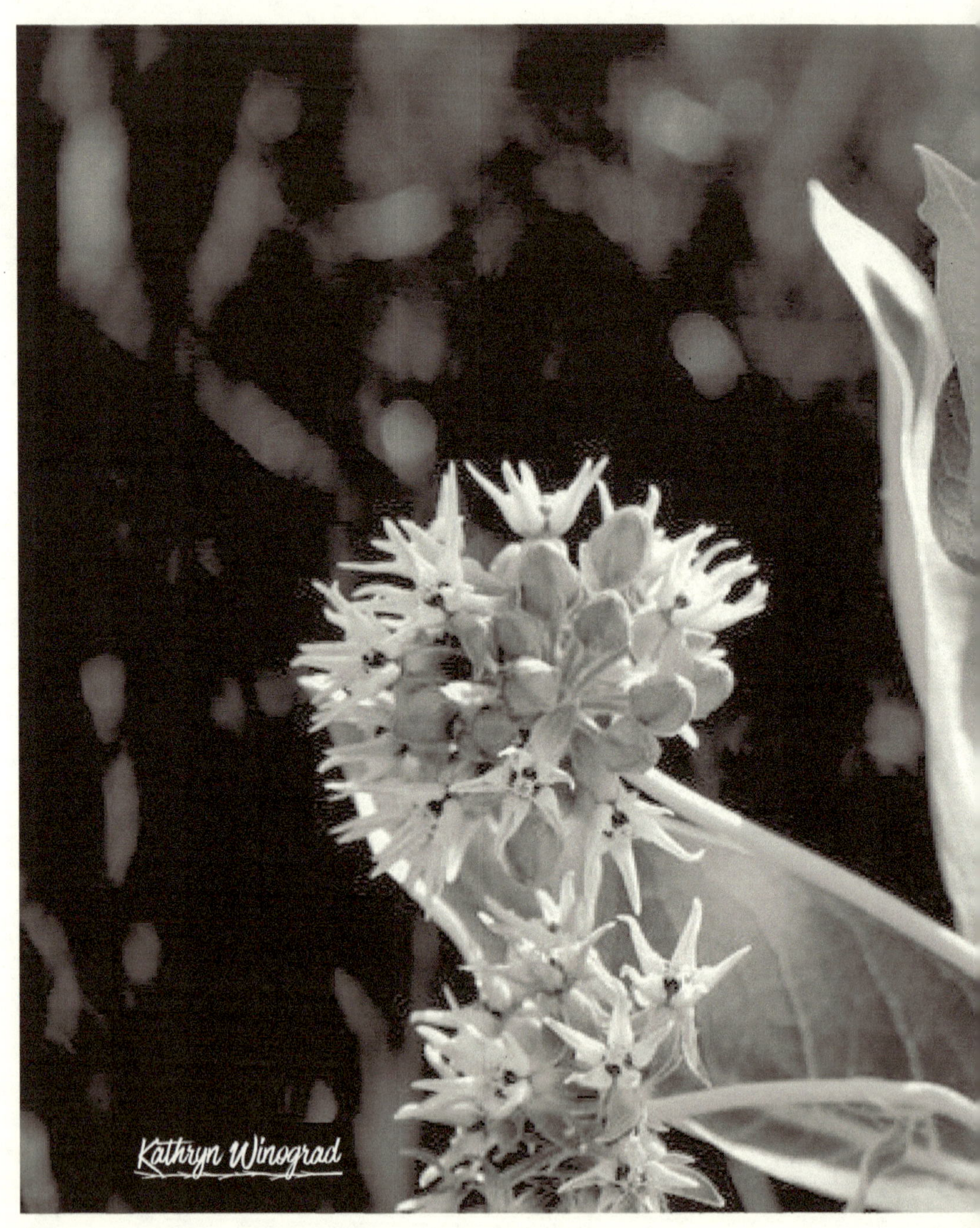
Kathryn Winograd

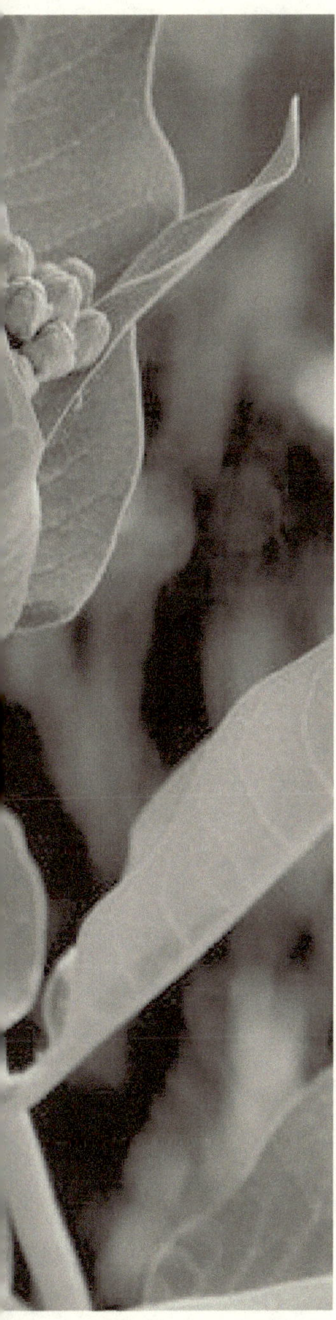

Powdered sugar love song
Black and yellow bands
Competing for Apollo
throughout all the lands

Sunflowers stretch
towards guillotine skies
Daisies bright
Marigolds with feathery eyes

Winter encroaches
gaze shifts
Lovers with little daggers
stuck between ribs

Royal flushed cheek
pressed to windowpane
Open the mind's eye
Refocus without shame

Marigolds
Stephanie Lamb

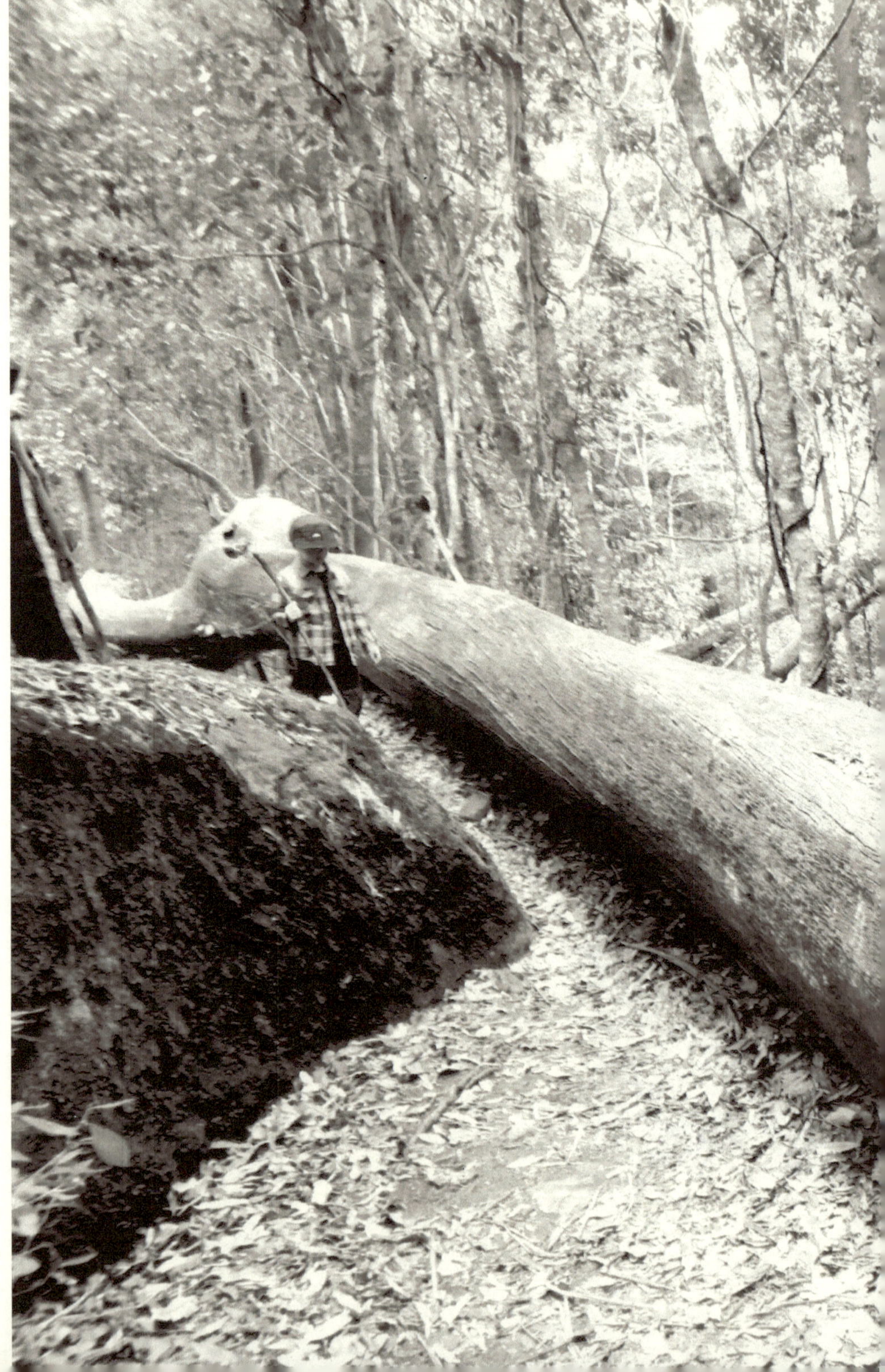

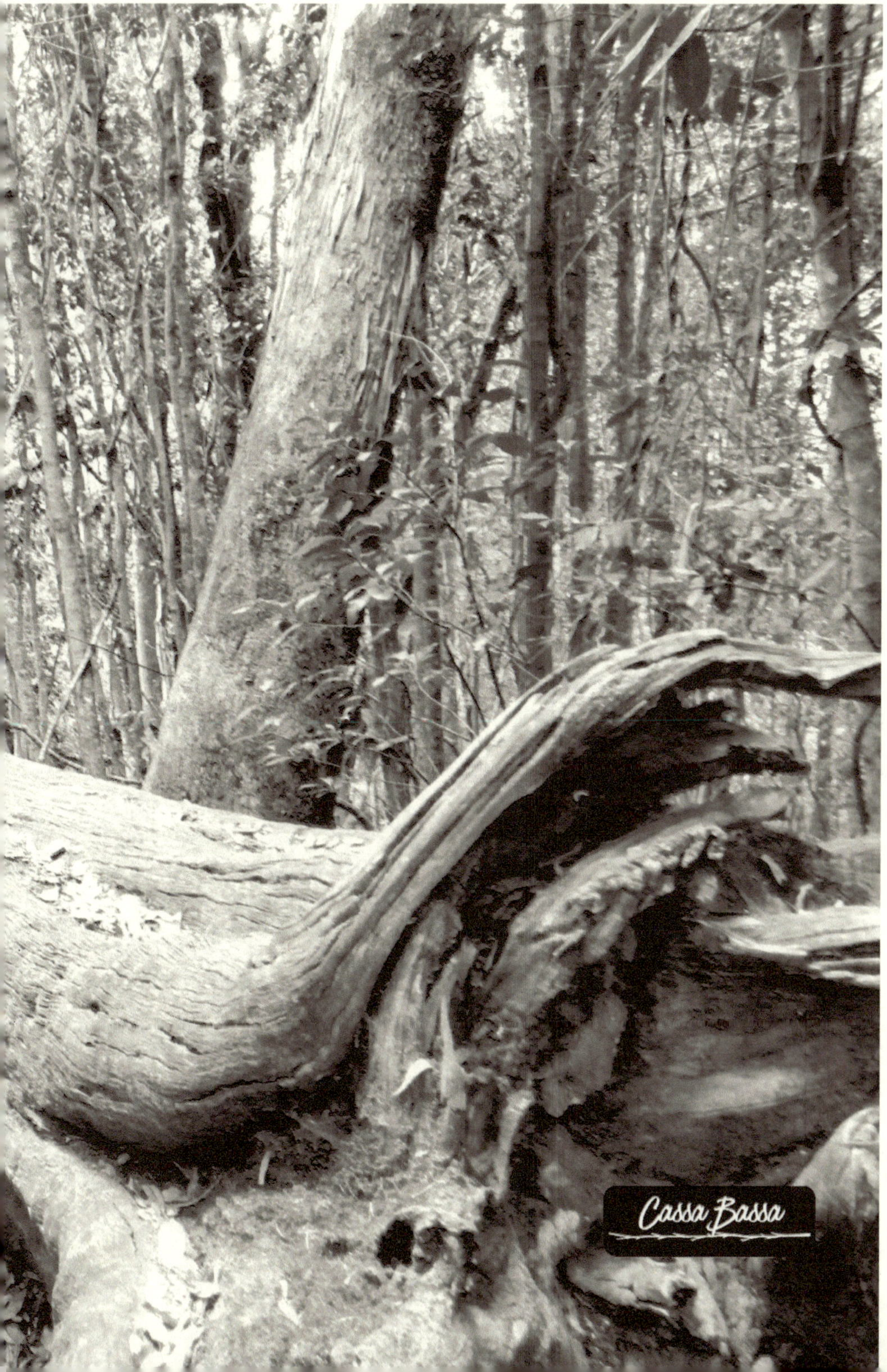
Cassa Bassa

he is quiet and reserved
enjoys the company of
trees and wild plants
birds and insects
are his family

he tells the time
by the shadows of the woods
he knows danger
by its sound
he nurtures his soul
by going deeper and deeper
into the forest

he wears moonlight
dances by the fire
sings over the wildflowers
sleeps in the cradle of
the jungle

he is a forest child
full of vitality
harmony
and
enigma

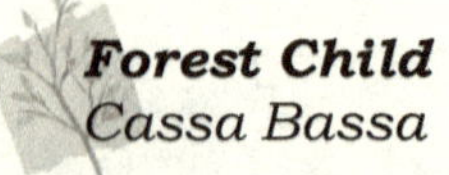

Forest Child
Cassa Bassa

I'm locking this moment away, little bird.
There will come a time that you'll
require less of me, and this is all
I'll have left to hold.
This precious hour in
the shadow of a great maple,
an ancient observer,
you lay against my chest
as we slowly swing.

My Fathers spirit dancing in
the branches above us,
I prayed to recognize
this moment, little bird,
to appreciate its arrival.
To glimpse an existence
unencumbered by
the knowledge
of our impermanence.

I'm locking this moment away, little bird.
I'm locking it
into place where
I can always find you
in the shadow of the great maple,
waiting to remind me
that love transcends
the demise of these earthly bodies,
and dances in the trees.

Waiting for us to remember
that we, too, have cause to dance.

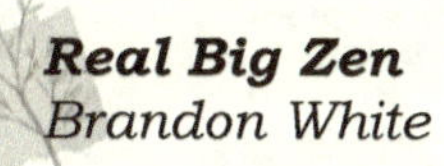

Real Big Zen
Brandon White

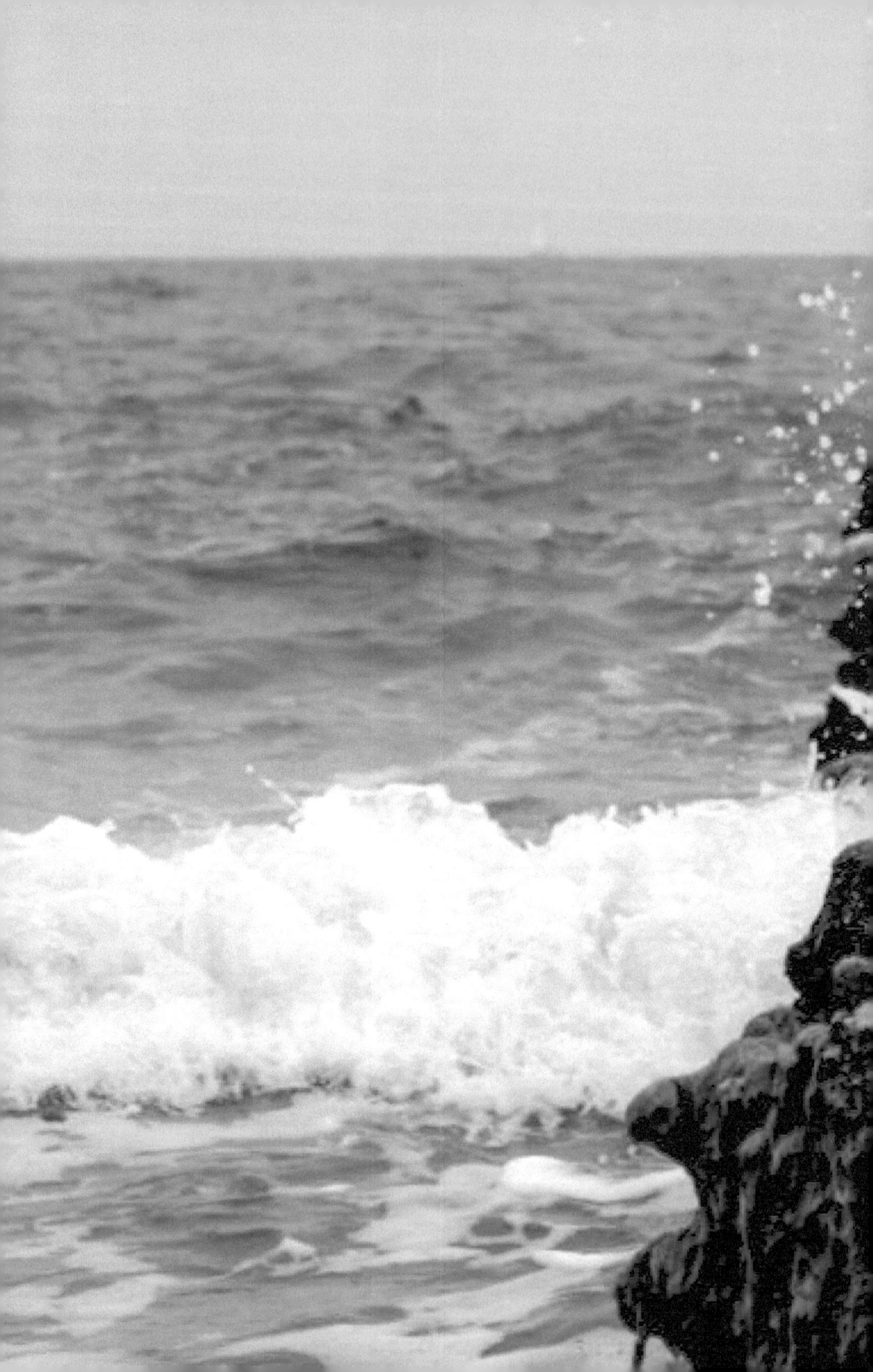

BLUE EARTH

The waves, the waves,
glow with Moon's rays.

Hiding the depths,
from the light of day.

The lurking beasts scream
against the water weight
of one thousand earths
in the crushing place.

Feed and feast
on the lesser beasts,

while the lurkers eat,
the moonlight seeps
into the dark,
as pearls that gleam.

Sinking deeper,
the light, it creeps,
and puddles in beads
around the feet
of lurking things
that wish to feed…

silent and lightless,
mindless and starved,
those ancient teeth
pierce the cold meals
that true darkness brings.

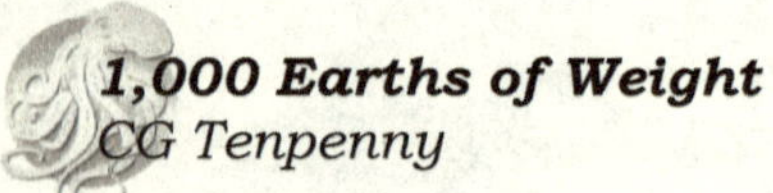

1,000 Earths of Weight
CG Tenpenny

The sea sings to me
Her soft voice as sweet as honey
As gentle as the caress
Of the new moon's glow,
Wanders over the fields and plains
Now parched, now washed
In the moistness of her tear-fall pull,
Plays through the valleys
Like a child
Naked, new and free,
And still she sings,
Rises over the scree and slate
Lifting me like a promise
Like a prayer,
High through the pastel-blue
Where her children dance
Silent beneath the hypnotic hum,
Beyond the ox-bow and the fall
Her voice ebbs and flows
But never falters
Never fades,
As through the wistful glade,
Dappled like the willow
Its branches bowed in reverence,
It kisses the stream which flows
Like quicksilver through my veins,
Washes me clean from source to mouth
And sings to me
Her song of hope.

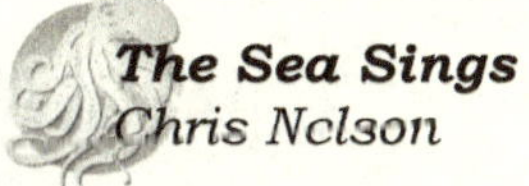

The Sea Sings
Chris Nelson

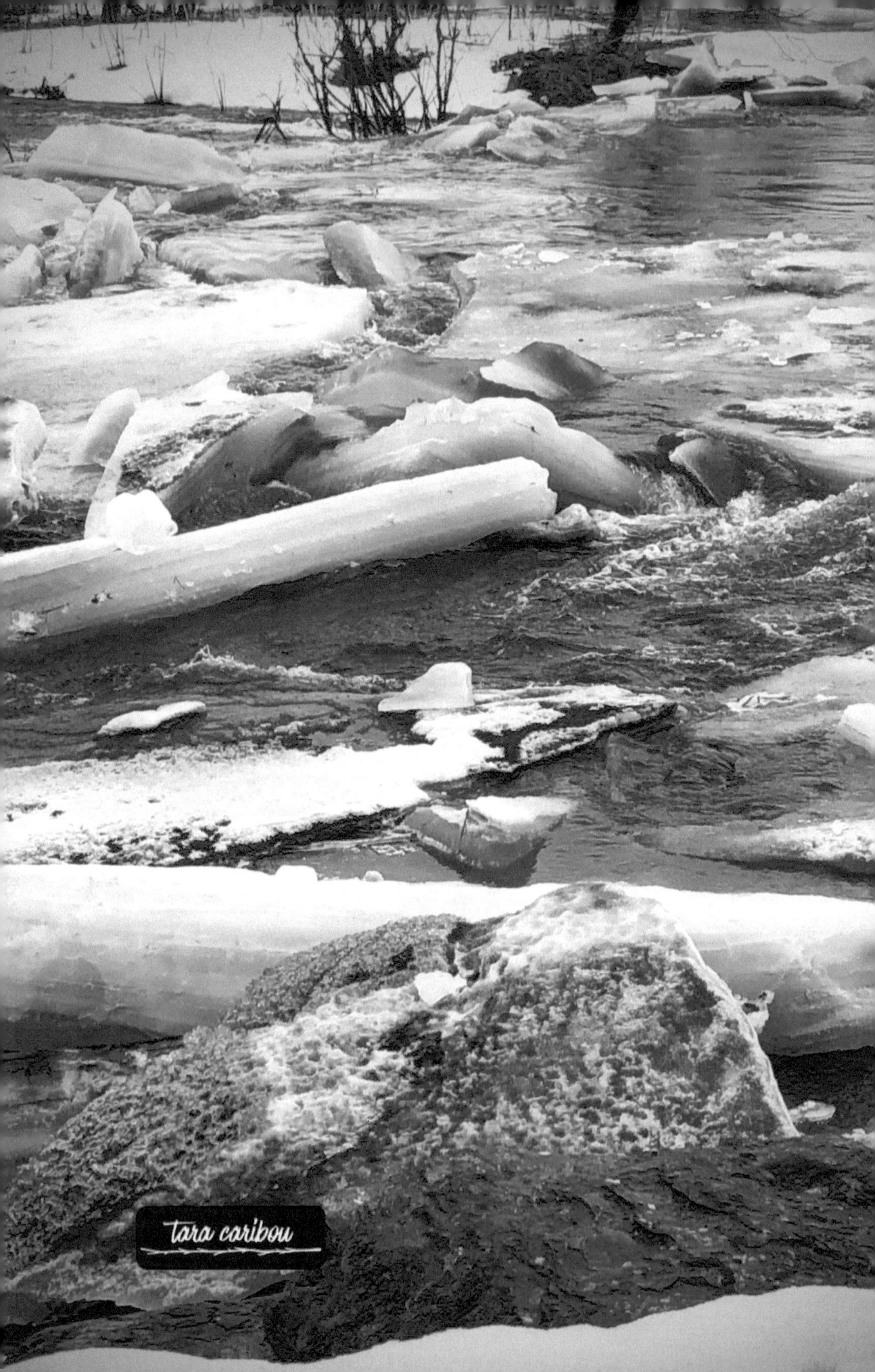
tara caribou

A river may sprout from a beautiful spring,
Just like love, when it first weathers your heart.
Forging a place for shelter and promise.
Allowing love's stream to make a fresh start.
Even along the river's course,
We treasure our memories of the source.

A river's stretch is not judged by length,
The ripples, nor the weaving.
Changes convey resilience,
Preventing us from leaving.
There is always some resistance,
But we see a future in the distance.

As we depart into the vast ocean,
We consider the high velocity.
When the course comes to an end,
We truly find reciprocity.
We long for times of second chances,
And, of course, our first advances.

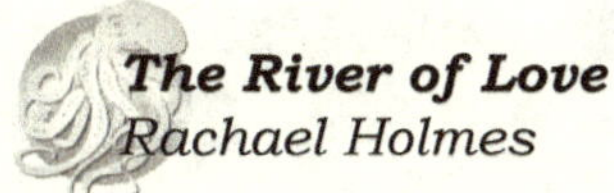

Here on the wild, west coast,
near the great continent's southern-most tip,
rest a while.

Here Eve's footprints marked the rocks,
her children decorated the caves and adorned their bodies
in shades of ochre and red.

Stretch out, open your mind,
feel the sun-warmed rock, absorb the stone-etched stories.
Isn't this the magic you're seeking?

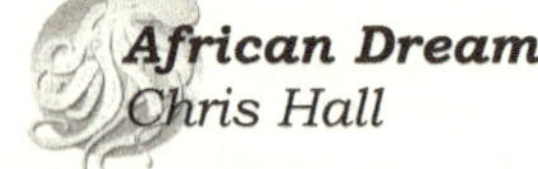

African Dream
Chris Hall

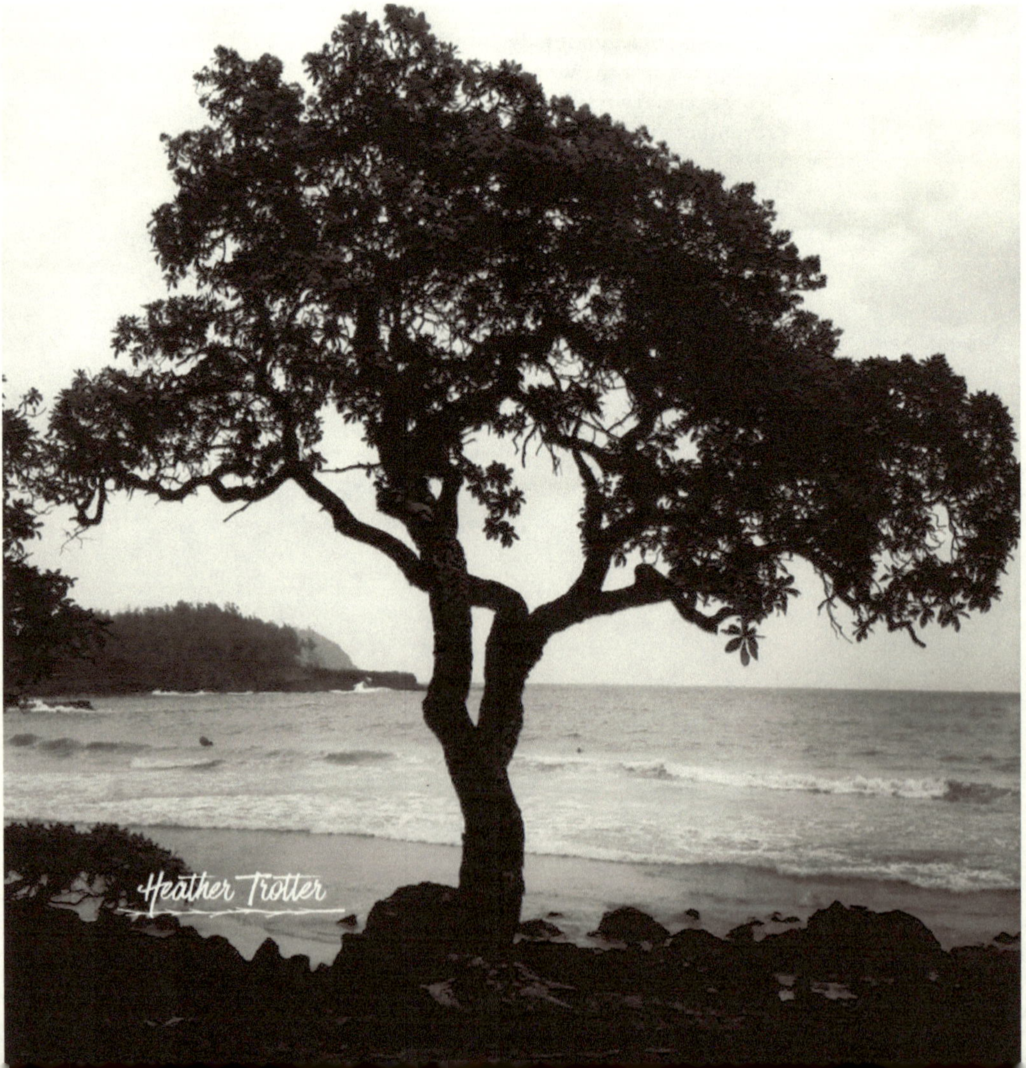

Heather Trotter

Dappled reflection
of palm trees
in cool waters
amid the chatter
of mallards,
curious egrets
and craving crows

How graceful
the birds swim
in the shallow inlet,
seeing their reflection,
looking deeply
into the soul
of its wavy nature.

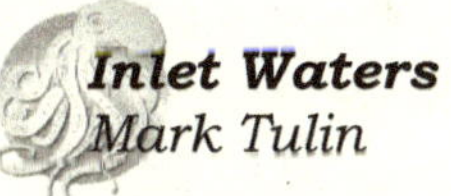

Inlet Waters
Mark Tulin

Groundling seas
flow from the peaks
of the Old Mother 'neath.

Snowy locks,
unbraided,
drift in the wind,
and,
as meltwater,
sink into the earth
again.

This is the endless dream.

Old Mother breathes
deeply,
and lulls
us back to sleep,
where we summit
her highest reaches
to watch our tears

freeze,
melt and flow
as one with
the infinite sea.

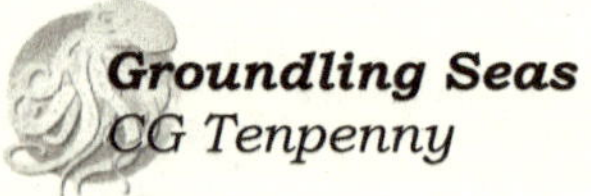

waves they crash me to and fro
rushing rifts they trap me
in this hard core ebb and flow
sea urchins circling, no deep sea lore
digging from the deep
leaving me gripping for fairest core

all the while...

sailboats in distance make love to the wind
as swells catch up to the horizon
with slow ascend
i ready for the course, hopeful
yet grim
unsure whether to dive
or simply jump in
i still my thoughts, looking to the shore
as buoyancy stares back at me
sand castles hiding there
sweet little testaments
whispering from the moor
these waves they still me
crashing this to and fro
til sensibility whispers, come
i'll show you just where to go....

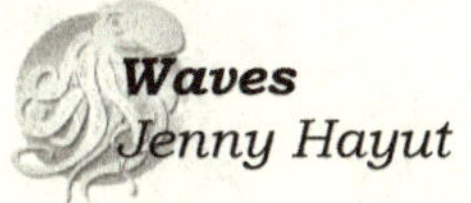

Waves
Jenny Hayut

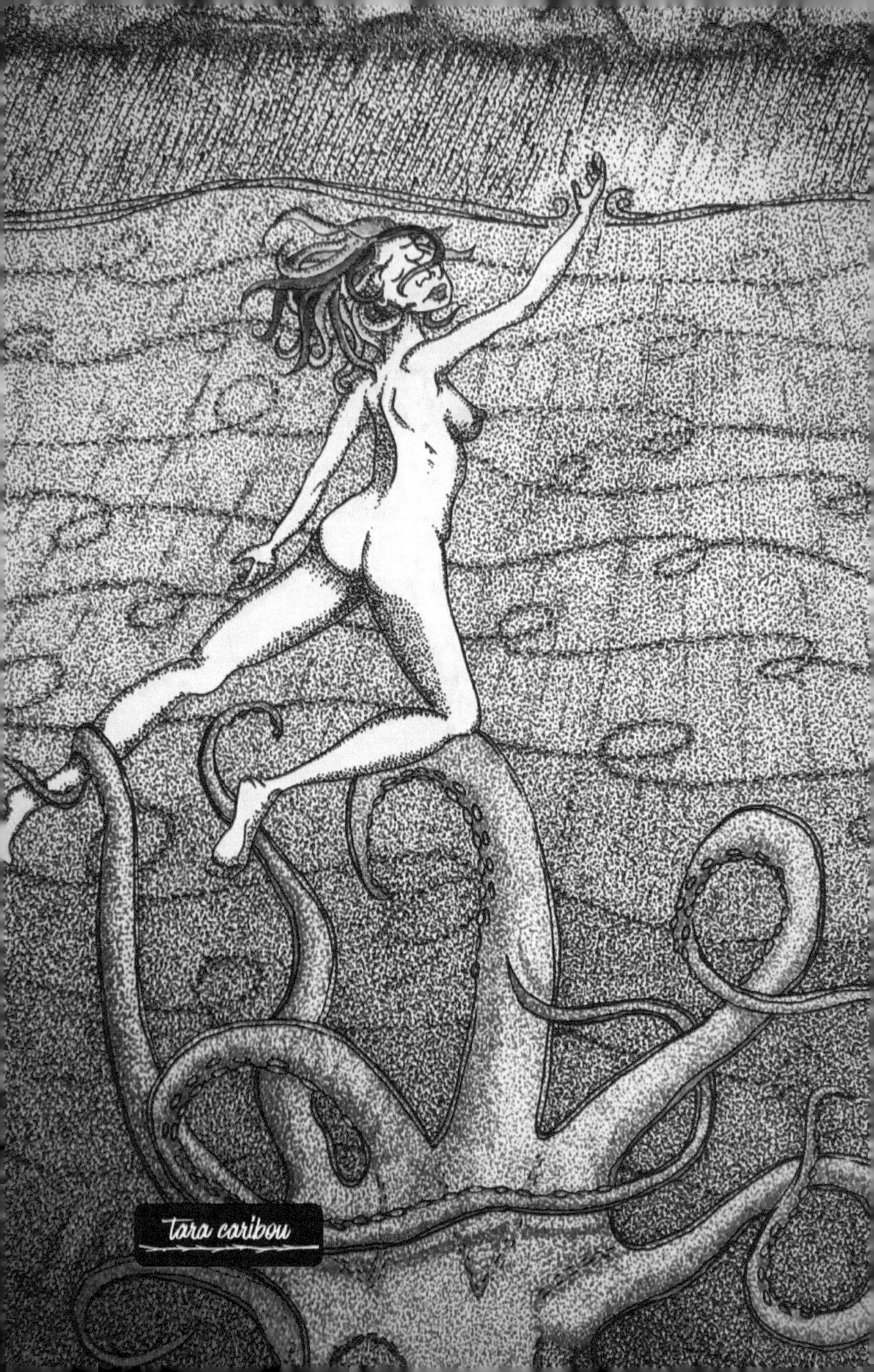
tara caribou

And all is calm and still
But for breaking waves on sand
Far-flung fingers of the sea
Grasping at the wretched land

Stretching toward the one she loves
With desperate, longing, lustful hands
Throwing herself against the shore
Where on the beach, there walks a man

He feels her tears in spraying brine
The tide goes out, he hears her sigh
In every wave, her yearning whimper
In every storm, her vengeful cry

Her passion was like a hurricane
Her ardor, wild and unbound
He, a mortal, had but one choice
Leave, or by her love be drowned

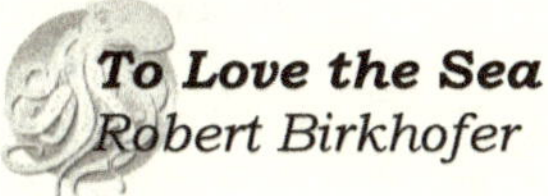

In the blackness,
a million fathoms deep,

she sleeps

in a pool
of the blackest ink,
coiled beneath

the ancient
and crumbling shell
of a fathom-dweller
slain by the waves,
in an age before
salt filled the sea.

She breathes in the silt
and exhales a wish –
the bubbles rise
toward the light,
so distant,
to share her dreams
and the bountiful gifts
that darkness
always brings with it.

But they never answer
and she remains

alone
in the deep,
beneath her shell.

Tears pool…
her blackest ink.

A Reminder to Sol

To what end
do the stars shine?

Old Luna glows
as a reminder to Sol
that too much heat
will hurt the whole.

Old Sun cries,
and wishes death –
a call for the coming
of blackness. Rest

in the absence of light,
the result of his burning
too brightly, this death,
by his own hand.

The stars would cry
at the loss
of one of their own,
and Luna would dimly glow…

the last of Sol's light shone
upon her cheeks,

"As the cold grows,
I know that I am eternally
alone."

When distant lights
give up their hopes,
Luna and her sisters
will roam
the emptiness,

forever and on.

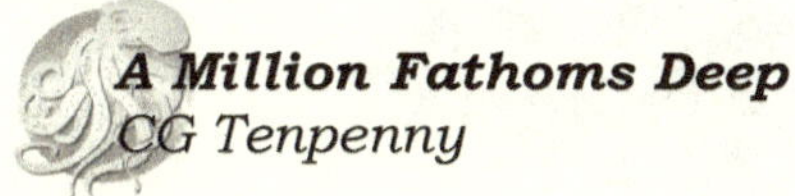

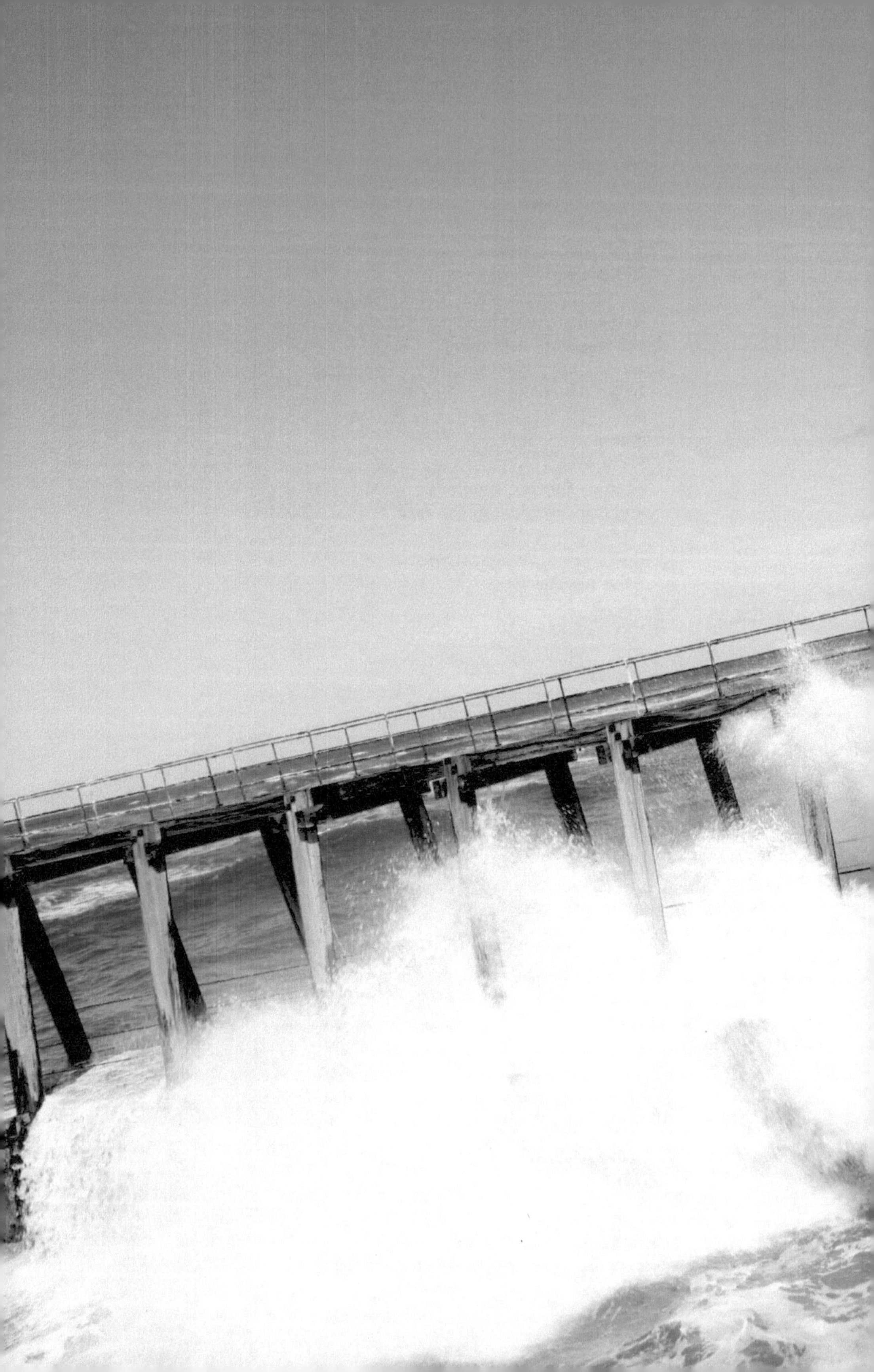

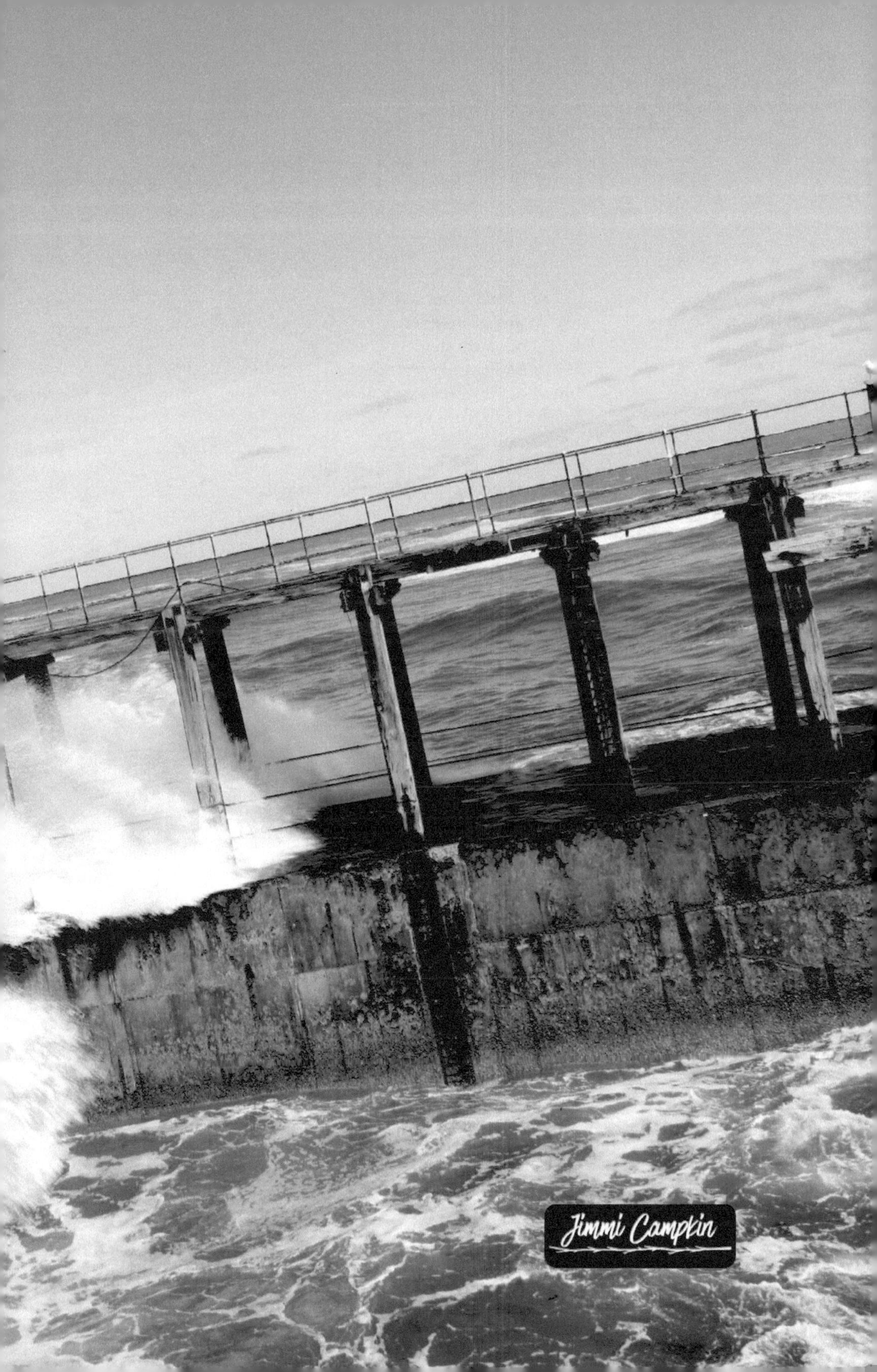
Jimmi Campkin

All I see around me
are curtains of bubbles,
plumes of azure sparks,
life swimming between my gloves,
around my fins in lazy circles,
circles of life from kelp
lounging on my leg to fish
glaring at the creature with no gills,
bubbles spurting from her tubed mouth.

Life is peaceful in orbit,
placement below another,
above the sandy weeds,
cycles, water ebbing, flowing
algae through my hair, blessed green
filaments staining me whole.

Less known than the moon
we gaze at from below,
levels, cycles ago from crescent
to gibbous to now entrenched
in light below water, glowing
bioluminescence my lantern
beneath the stars, under the shore.

My curtain thickens, blinding
eyes unwilling to look down,
only beyond the murky waves,
pieces, fragments of time, stone
shapes emerging, bones, life
without the heat of sun, light
of day at the tops of cycles,
burned by a fiery core.

The shore calls me,
air my home away from sea
where curtains sink to the floor
not rise like tides, rushing,
pushing fish aside, pulled
by moons, unstable, perfect
asynchronism. I feel unsteady
with continuity, land beneath my feet,
above the fish who cycle me.

Minutes more, I say,
hours before I taste salted air,
feel wind rustle my hair,
wash the kelp away, a cycle
ended with forceful fingers,
so just seconds more, a bit more
life, gilled, clinging to plastic fins,
a bit more bubbles, shrouding
the sea in shimmering light,
a just bit
more.

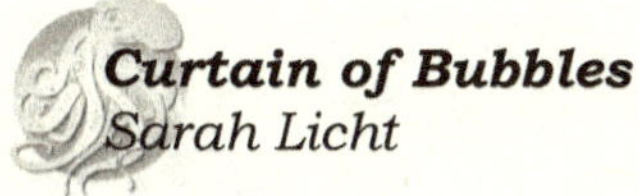

Curtain of Bubbles
Sarah Licht

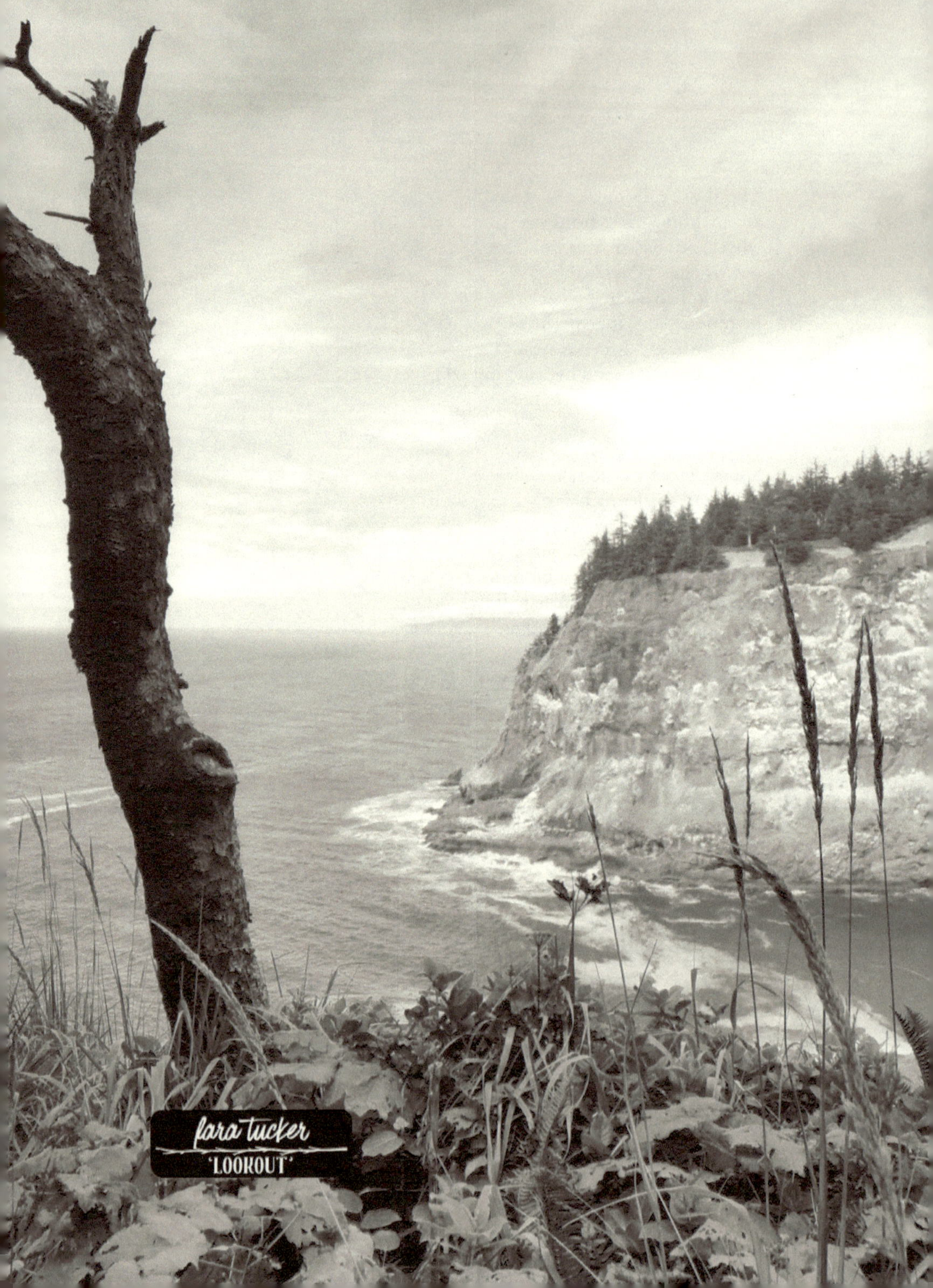
fara tucker
'LOOKOUT'

We stand on the shore, called down by the ocean.
The sweet swell motions the blood.
Reminds me I am human.
I feel safe in this storm.
As the wind rushes these bones.
Threatening the inevitable damage.
I wait for the change.
Holding out for such wild destruction.
This land knows me not, we are but visitors here.
Collecting coconuts of contempt that we store for every season.
Each man an island. Each one built on sand.
Atlantis parading in peril.
Off on the horizon the ship struggles.
Souls shuffle, towards that great divide.
For that I cry.
But the tempest suffocates.
Throws away my tears, out into the eye that hovers.
And weeps only painful laments.
God watching on, lifting no finger.
Remembering the flood.
Soon we are drowning, smashed by the waves.
Broken on the shore of our lives that already began to recede.
I crawled once from the sea.
And too it now, we have returned.
Scattered and in pieces.
Littering the ocean floor.

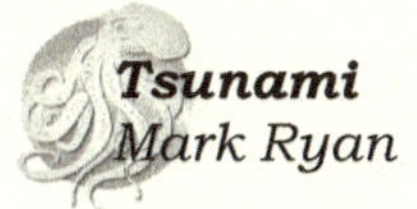

Tsunami
Mark Ryan

Here in the dark,
at the edge of the wood,
a tear from the Mother
flows from the mud

and into the sea,
to twist in the salt,
where it folds
with the waves,
and sinks
to the heart.

Mist and cold kisses –
missed, the Wind wishes
for a second chance to whistle
her hymn, hissing,
the hymnal's page flips,
as the gilded edge gleams
brightly from within
the evening's
mist.

The midnight oaks,
blessed to be so old,
wait and watch
her lips,
whispering
a secret, a hint,
a treasure, pursed
and pressed against
the shore,
where the waves

rumble
rumble

for all they are worth,
until Luna begs
their silence.

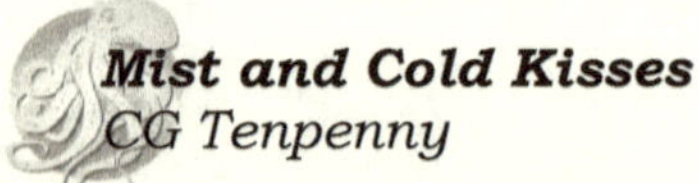

In the darkness of the dawn
by the waterfall where wet curtains meet
she tiptoes over slippery rocks
singing softly to rising ripples.

In the cool of the morning
peals of giggles ring out like raindrops
as she drops her dress and lifts her face
to whirl in liberated circles.

In the heat of the afternoon
she dives through silver sheets
into the limpid pool below
where herons dart and fishes swim.

In the shade of the evening
she floats among sunlit shadows
surrounded by scented petals
cloaked in azure calm.

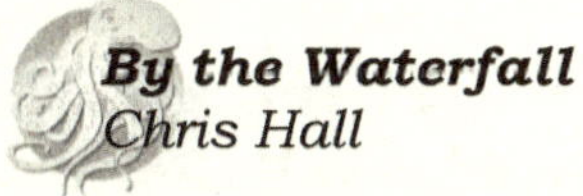

By the Waterfall
Chris Hall

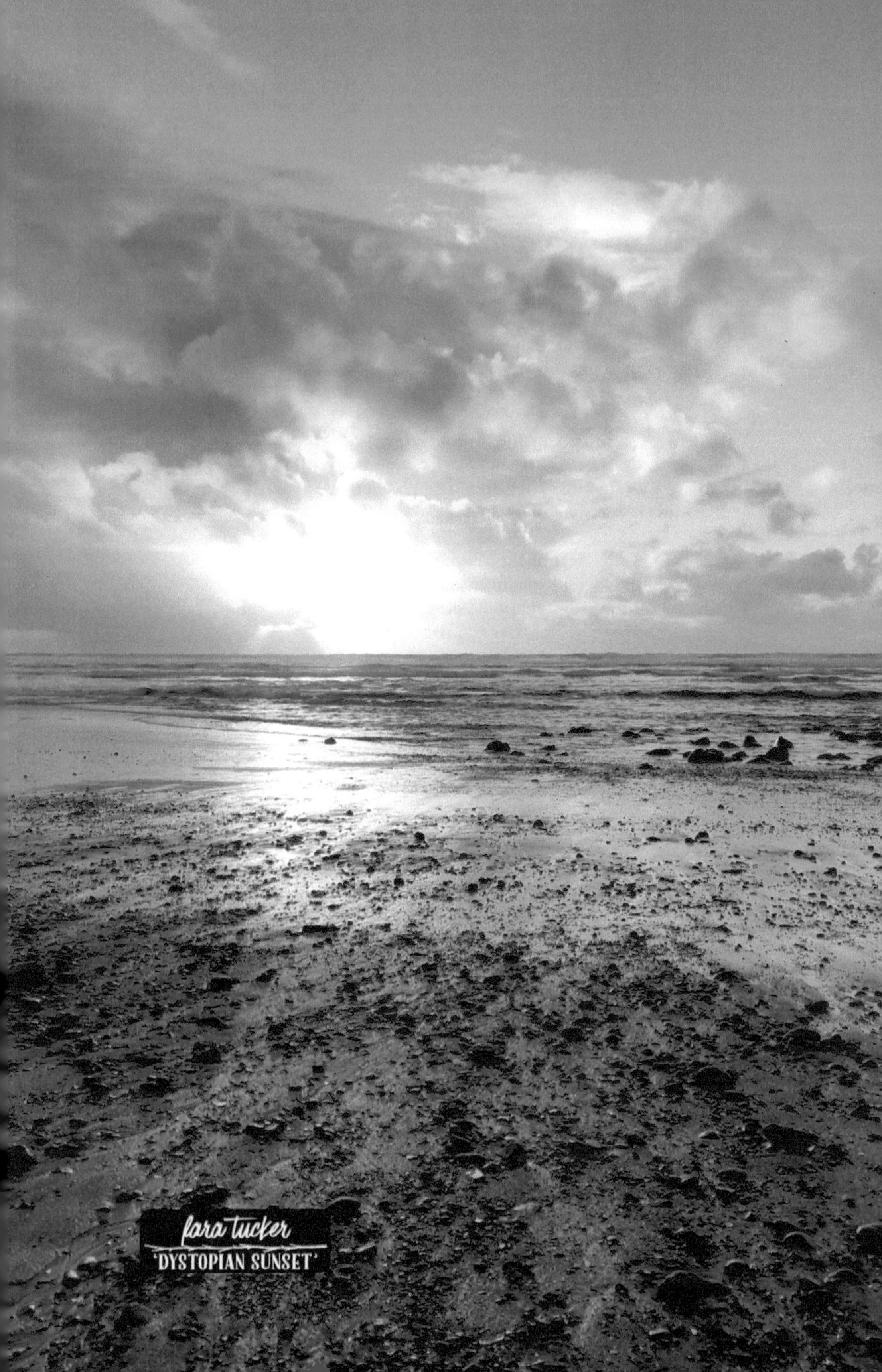
fara tucker
'DYSTOPIAN SUNSET'

We used to go down to sea
Do you remember?
Back when we were more beasts than people

The sea is an insatiable writhing mass of longing
Oh, it would strip you flesh from bone, skin from soul
We sat among the shifting sands and echoed its roars

We licked salt sprays off the hollows of our hands
The tears of our ancestors, do you hear them singing still?

We buried our wildness here, our untamable girlhood
We slit its throat and let it bleed into the white laced water,
We shed our hides and bite our tongues
And with a mouth full of copper
We repeat, be tame, be sweet, be still

But sometimes when I dream, the sea calls to me still
Let go, let go, you are still too young
My shame silences me but a part cries
I shall, I shall, I shall

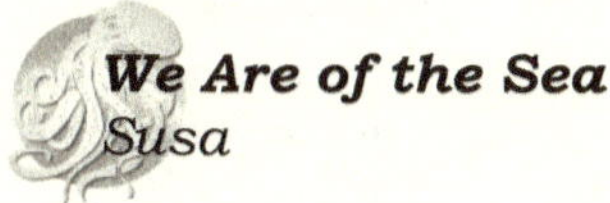

We Are of the Sea
Susa

Who is this beauty
drifting toward me?

She sways like kelp,
pushed by the waves.

Help me!

She snaps like reeds,
blown by breezes
coughed from the throats
of deep sea beasts,
as if Old Kraken
rose, crested,
and then sneezed.

Crystal-shine from ice,
crusting her scaly smile
of northern seas.

Oh God…
how her heat freezes.

Pale skin,
the corpse-thing,
lacking oxygen...
dead, unfeeling,

she is blue,
corpse eyes
are slowly blinking,
but...

she's sunken
and I'm sinking.

I put my hands against
her shoulders
to push away,
retreating,
but her jagged-coral
fingertips
leave slits

in my throat
where the tiniest fish
can swim and play,
and laugh while feasting.

Then I realized
that she was not
a thinking thing,
nor even a 'she',
but a mindless creature
of the deep,

whose ink and spots
would flow and leak
to mimic a thing

that would cause
no second thought,
nor the slightest pause
as I offered myself

for it to eat.

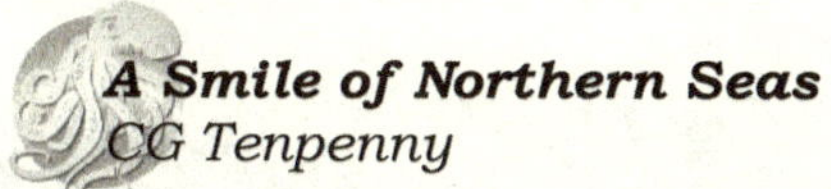

A Smile of Northern Seas

CG Tenpenny

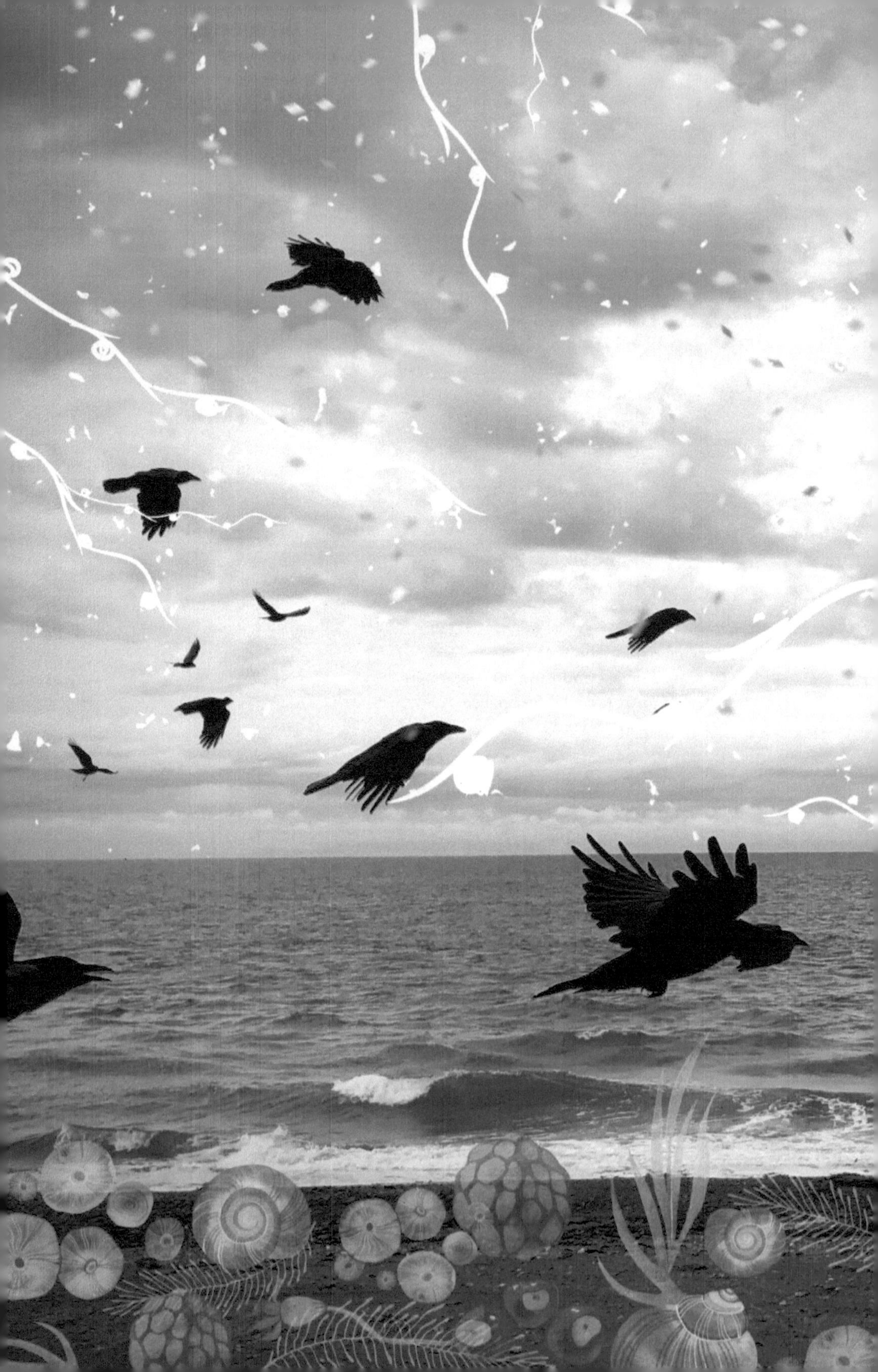

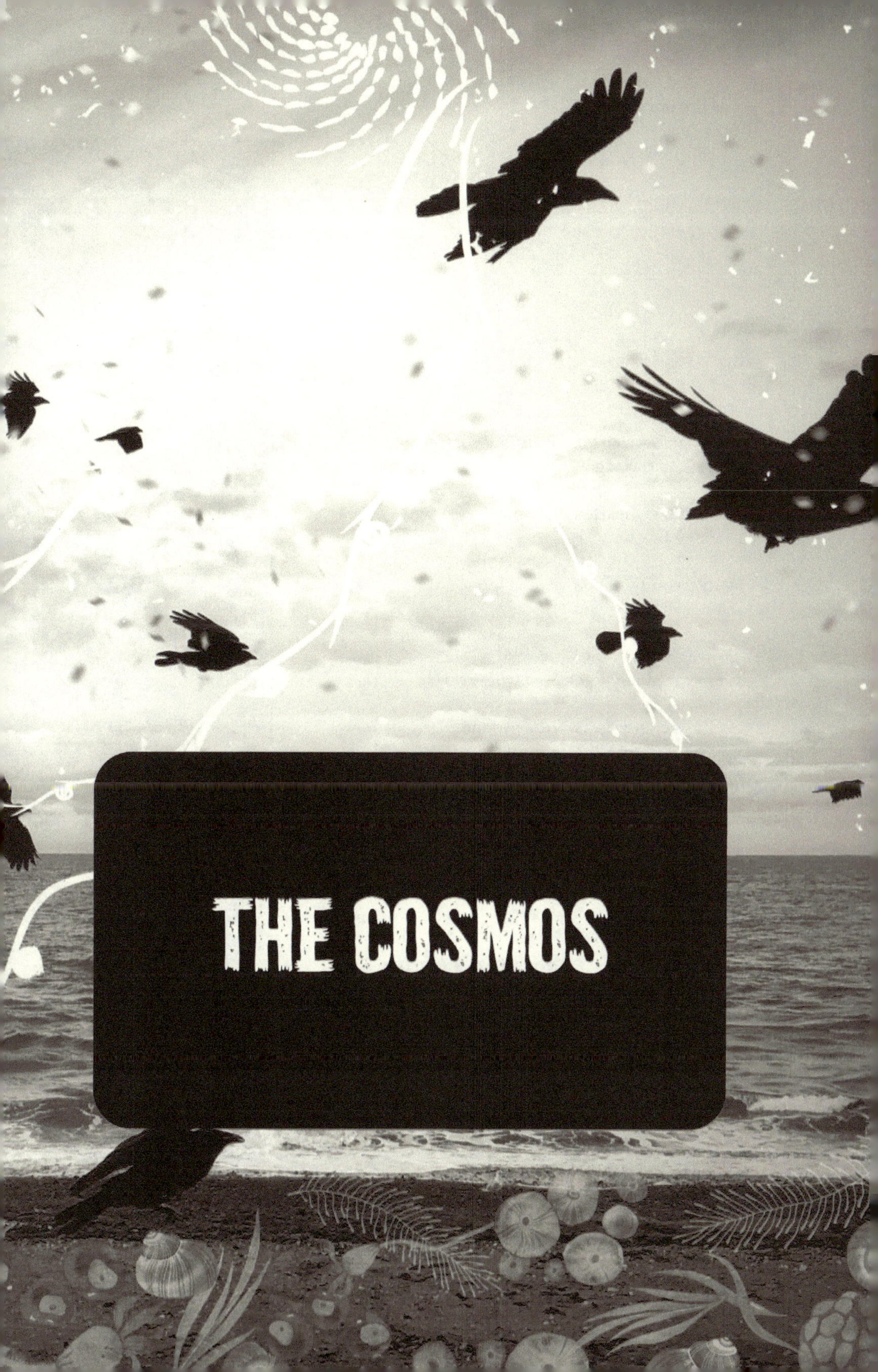
THE COSMOS

The sparrow sings her morning song
with no knowledge

of the heavy-hearted man
listening below.

Would you fly if you were able?
I sure as hell wouldn't.

To see that far down the road
is not the ability to change where it leads.

So I'll keep my feet on the ground,
and be grateful

that the things of the sky
return with songs of hope.

Together we watch the sun
set the horizon to burning.

Regarding Flight
Brandon White

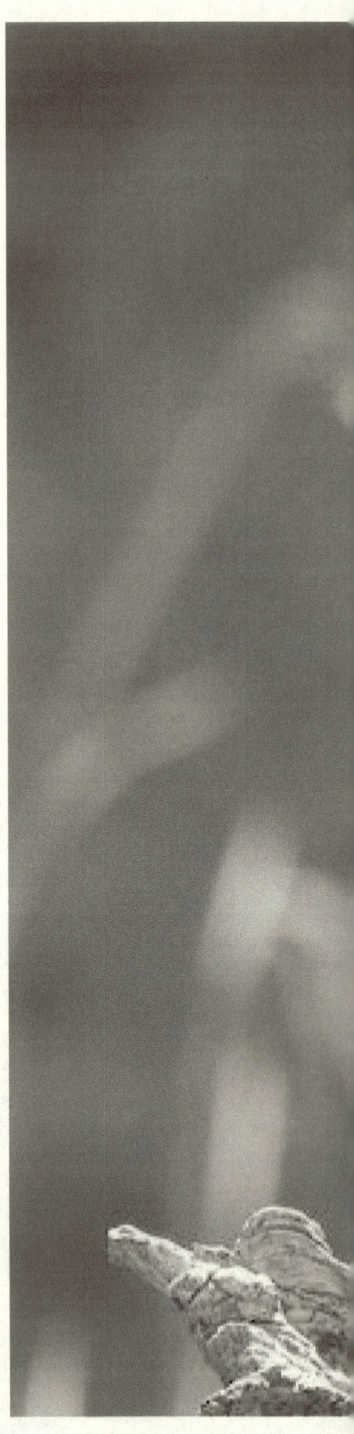

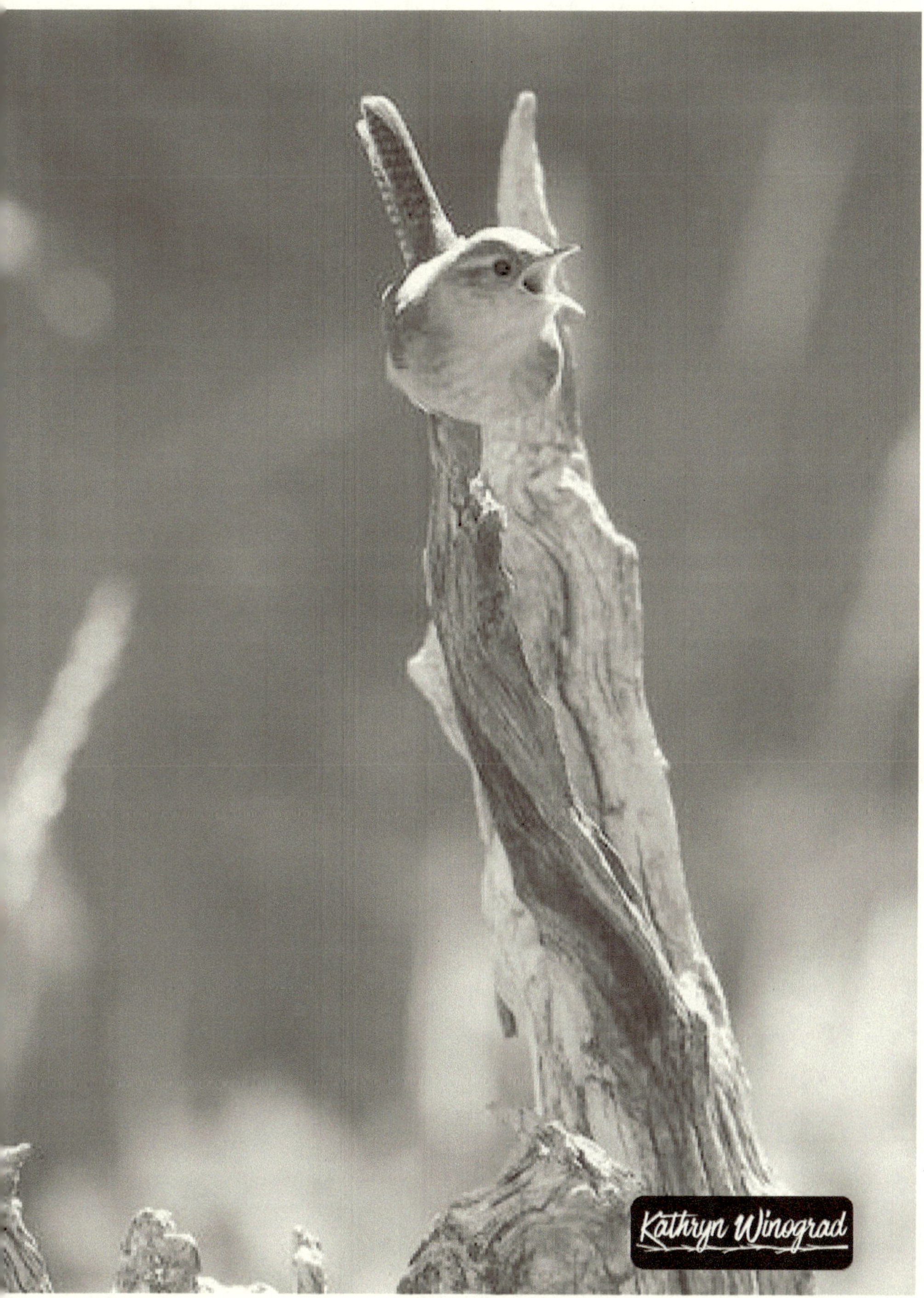
Kathryn Winograd

Your clouds are black.
Coffee stained and lava grey.
Swirling and destroying like a tornado touching down.
Soaking me in rain dripped misery.
Sucking the bolts from my foundation.
There's no calm in your storm.
No eye to your needle of chaos.
Swelling your seas in the face of my defiance.
Shouting into the winds of your frustration.
But you are just a raging storm.
Swelling and ebbing like the tides to the moon.
Lost in my lonely hurricane.

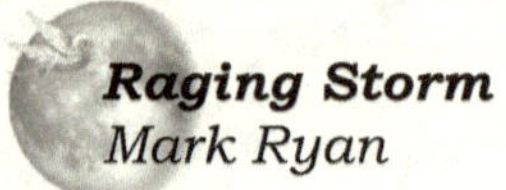

Raging Storm
Mark Ryan

From the dust we're born,
Rumored to return once more,

Enigmatic energy boiling from below,
Reaping repercussions of unbearable cold,

Baby blue tears raining above,
Washing away bodies of blood,

Endless seas of salt and silt,
Dry and deserted where mountains filled,

Bolstering breezes of wild wingless wind,
Pressurized plumes spew from each end,

Impeccable Ice shards scar the sky,
Watching warmth of one burning eye.

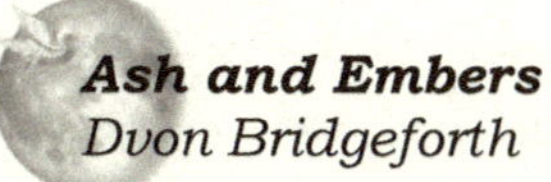

A single star casts insufficient light
Yet; transcends the dark around it

A black canvass to hold our despair
A thousand stars to hold our hope

Streaks of broken dreams burn, crashing
And though temporary; the light is brilliant

Tear drops mourning us, fixed in night sky
Stars; the monuments of hope's victory

Monuments
Hidden Bear

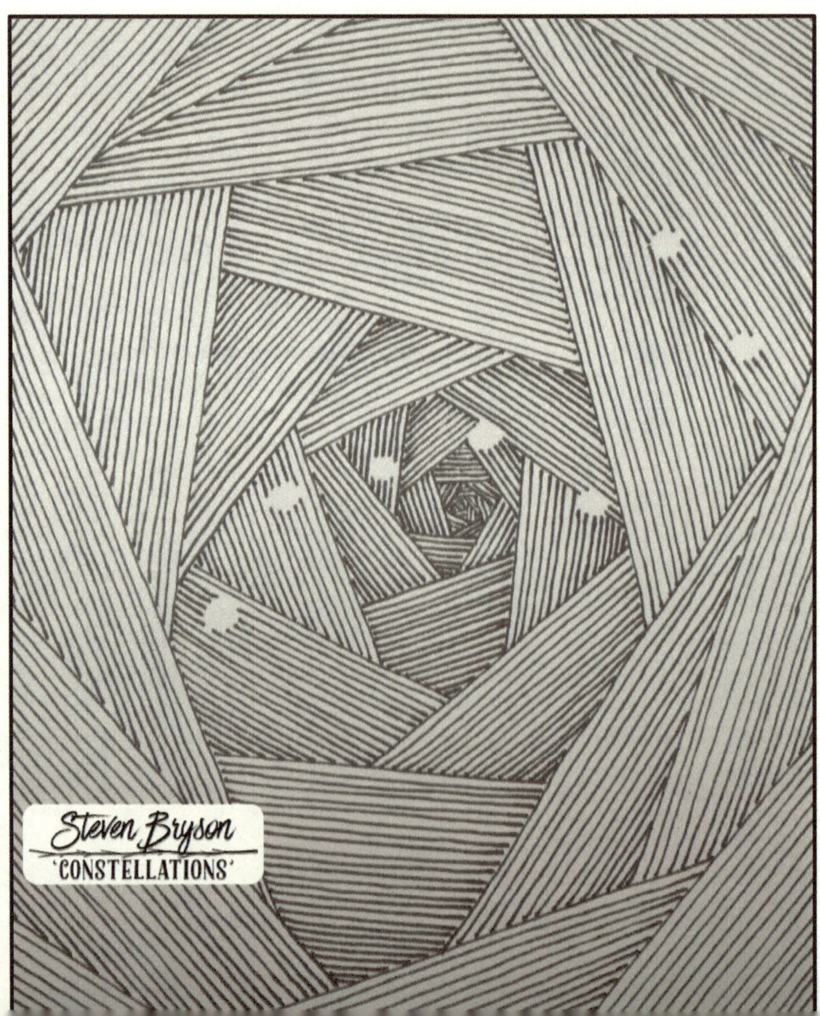

Snow small as rain
wanders past the dark firs
and pines, barely touches me.
So slow this waking, this
waiting. The first threads
of grass unravel beneath
tiny corridors of stone
and the cold wedges of elk
and deer hooves and the black
cows sold this winter,
which will not lay their calves
down again— small flowerings—
in the bare gullies to sleep.

This winter, I snow-shoed
through the wind-carved shadows
of blue trees, drove
past glittering ice rivers,
wild geese quiet on wet stones,
deer in the road ditches,
frost-feathered, unafraid.

Soon, the gold banner
and the purple iris shall
riddle these fields, and the pink
geraniums rise, and the boulder raspberry
float from winter dark crevices
through the deep woods and the wild
gardens, white as the snow
when we could touch anyone.

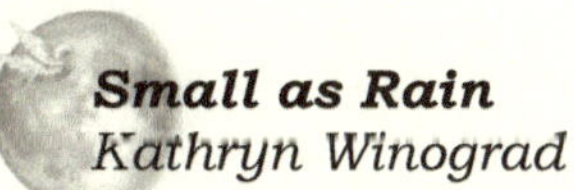

Small as Rain
Kathryn Winograd

The earth hangs above,
a ball indistinguishable
from a meadow of stars,
its blue oceans stained yellow,
iodized rays of light
from light traveled years
to reach my eyes.

If I reach out,
I can see the swirling clouds,
the cities lost in optical translation
crush between my fingers,
blinking and weaving
in and out,
out and in.

Small enough for fingers
to turn its mountains to dust,
yet vibrant and strong enough
for rays of yellow light
to reach the ground I stand on.

It stands small and insignificant,
and yet,
from light years away,
so do I.

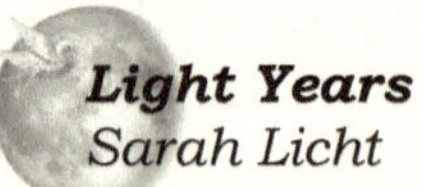

Light Years
Sarah Licht

A multitude of you in the sky,
The vast heavens you dignify;
What do you do when you're up there?
Lively banter and laughter share?
So many things I want to know;
Do you desire for simply glow?

Does empathy move freely there?
A dying star to mourn and care;
Or envy the one that shines the brightest,
Sway your gowns see who's the finest;
Are you engaged in a race for fame?
What makes you burn your inner flame?

Does a cloudy night steal your peace?
Or rest and breathe a sigh of relief;
Did shooting stars fall from that height?
Or were they drawn to our kitchen lights;
On nights when there's so less of you,
Are you singing praises in the pew?

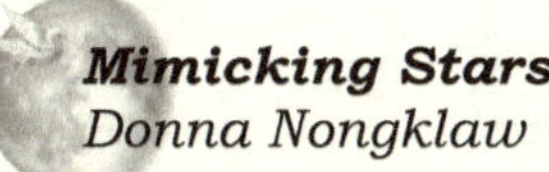

Mimicking Stars
Donna Nongklaw

I am one of those people
who spends hours on cloud watching
as if heaven is the storyteller
with dramatic illustration to its
enchanted audience

Aladdin sits on the flying carpet
cascading down the marble stairwells

The clown holds up colored cotton candies
to the ferris wheel

Jelly fish swim towards
the horizon at sun set

Hot air balloons cruise above
the evening African safari
kites lost in the crushed dandelions

I am lost in a coma of visual fatigue

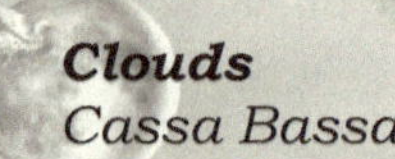

Clouds
Cassa Bassa

Jimmi Campkin

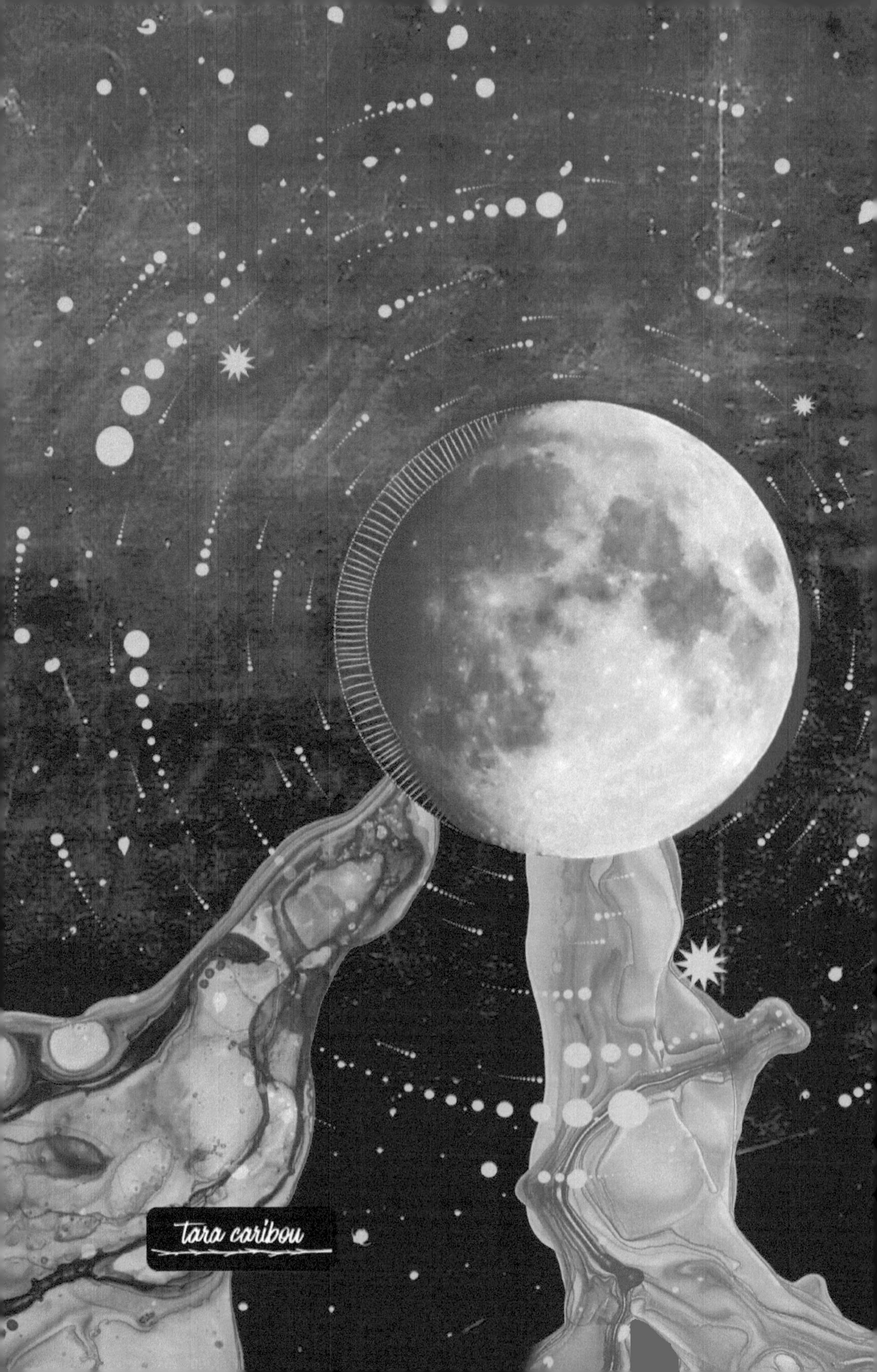
tara caribou

Staring at the x-rays of my metamorphosis
I'm sliding between my expedition and frozen inquisition
Caught in evanescent impressions
Vanishing in this discolored haze

As a consequence,
I'm bleeding a waterfall
Crying endlessly like a storm
Thunder playing over and over

In a trance magnetized to a silence
Cauterized by the blemishes I fail to see
Reminiscing of the turning point
Trace the wounds with a silver blade

As a consequence,
I'm bleeding a waterfall
Crying endlessly like a storm
Thunder playing over and over

Glaring at the anguish in a fog
I'm slithering between my transformation and ice cold retribution
Captured in a transparent disease
Disappearing in an empty smoke

As a consequence,
I'm bleeding a waterfall
Crying endlessly like a storm
Thunder playing over and over

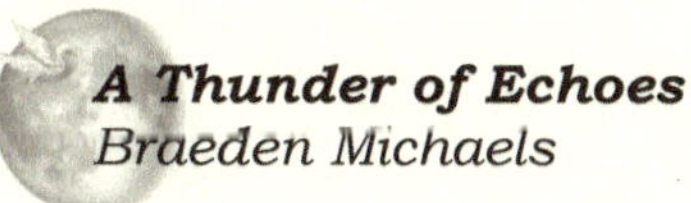
A Thunder of Echoes
Braeden Michaels

Imagine soaring upwards,
Against the downpour.
Feeling the water soak through,
Thrashing on our skin,
Drenching every pore.

Still we glide vertically,
In opposition with the storm.
Until we break through the clouds,
Entering a safe place,
Where only angels swarm.

Let us wait for the storm to pass,
Watch sand sprinkle in the hourglass.
Let us dream of tomorrow's solace.
When we can reclaim hope and promise.

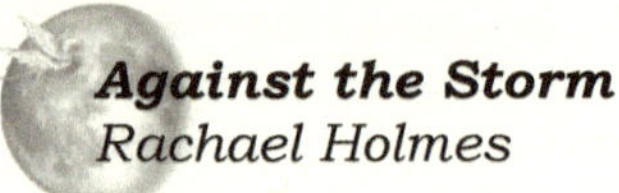
Against the Storm
Rachael Holmes

she smiles, peering from high above
her laughter, the breeze
upon the cheeks of men
even the mountain stretches forth to attain her

yes, her countenance
blesses all who touch her

her hair, feathering, white and radiant
on some mornings or
billowing and untamed
on some afternoons or
shadowed and crowned
in the sun's final light of the evenings

inclining her ear,
she harkens to the musings of the heavens
murmuring, she whispers wisdom below
an upward glance from the visage of men,
a faint movement of lips,
a prayer lifted:
desperation or defiance or damnation
or a request for deliverance
she observes and accepts impartially
yet with all tenderness

occasionally cleansing her spirit,
her tears dropping wherever they may:
mists of sorrow, downpours of purity
drizzling mediocrity, a deluge in fury

she has witnessed the movement of many
choked with debauchery
defiled by the corruption of would-be gods
ignored and worshipped

still she blesses and infuses her life
into theirs
spinning, always roaming, across
a landscape she will never step foot on

Vault of Heaven
tara caribou

My perch it is the highest fence
My view the clearest view,
I scan the city streets all day
In search of something new.

I watch the faces passing by
The frightened and the brave,
And steal their thoughts before they know
They're stumbling to the grave.

But never tree
Or hanging branch
Will ever hear me sing,

I move with grace
From left to right
But never on a limb.

I'll take the shiny and the dull
And keep them in my nest,
All the doors that never opened
Now locked inside my chest.

And when at night you cannot see
The memories that you lost,
I'll gaze upon each every one
And marvel at the cost.

But never will
I take the dive
Or sing out loud my song,

Just bob my head
From side to side
And pray that I'm not wrong.

I'll watch the Sun both rise and fall
And welcome day and night,
Basking in the cloak of darkness
And hiding in the light.

I'll never fly too far from home
For fear I'll lose my way,
Rather nest on stolen chances
As on my perch I stay.

So neither tree
Nor hanging branch
Will ever hear my song,

As safe I grasp
The middle ground
To be neither right nor wrong.

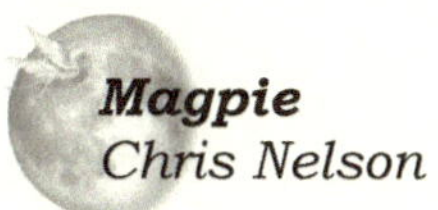

Magpie
Chris Nelson

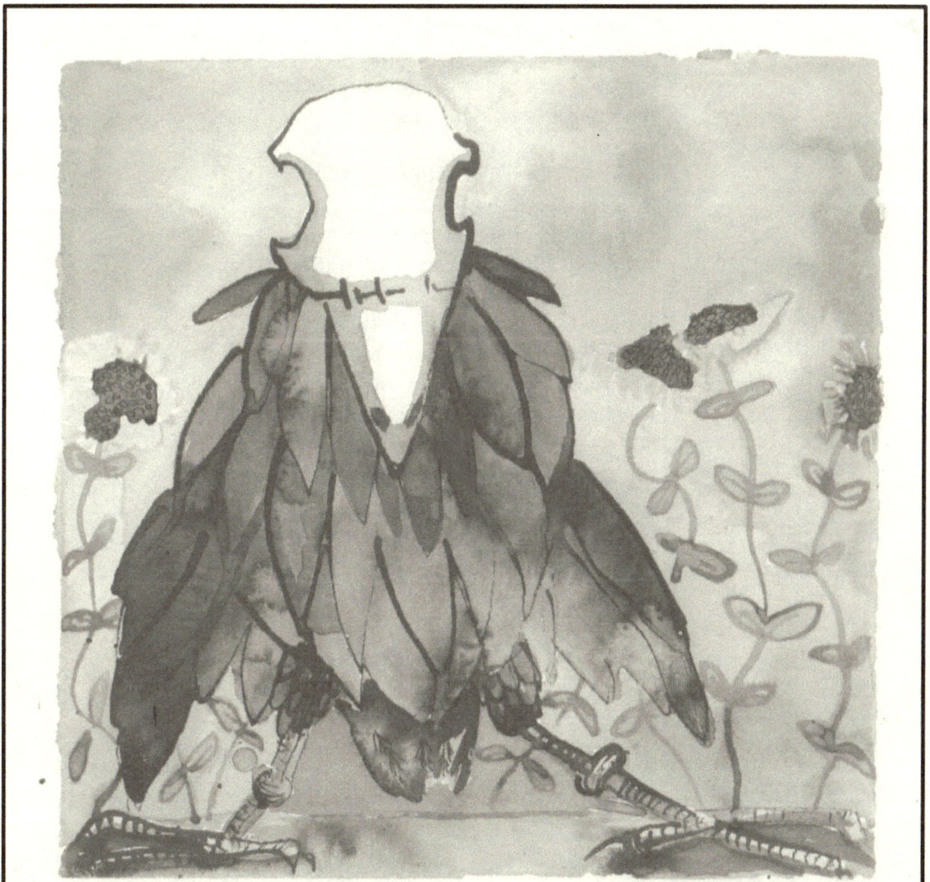

soul garden

emje
09-12-20

Hello Moon,
I think your wisdom is unparalleled,
Surveilling with eyes that are shriveled;
Grey and old, a quiet soul,
Like a sage in silvery stole.

Patience must be your strongest virtue,
From blackest nights you offer rescue;
You've seen them all, dynasties fall,
Heard your stories in many folklores.

If you spoke, what would you say?
Would you applaud us for our ways?
Or would I shudder when you explain?
The repercussions of our reign.

When you converse with God above,
Plead for those that labor for love;
For there are sins that hurt one soul,
And those which bloody tears unfold.

You must know all, you see the world,
One weighing scale is not for all;
Ask God to strike with mighty wrath,
The likes that pleasure in bloodbath,

Pray, don't scorn for wretched faults,
Life at times can be difficult;
Just as time imprisons you,
We are tied in shackles too.

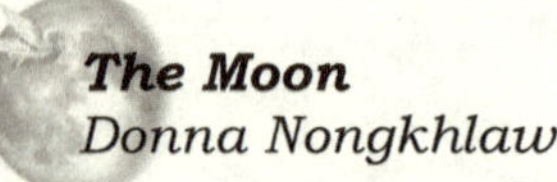

The Moon
Donna Nongkhlaw

Hawk Prince mounts highest spruce,
surveys coldly.

Trinkets jubilate beneath;
Flicking, flittering, tinkering, twittering;
cherry twigs entwine.

Hawk Prince dives, parting illuminated heavens;
Auburn bullet, piercing mist.

Soul cry shatters birdsong;
Visceral reverberation.

Trinkets, muted, scurry toward underbrush.

Hawk Prince, keeper of song, stifles melody.

Now he lies dead atop colored leaves,
Gleamless eyes.

Speckled tail feathers wind flutter.

The trinket-minded murdered him;
Damnation exchanged for a warbler's giggle.

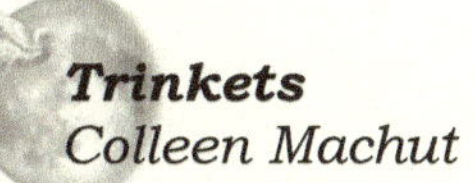

Trinkets
Colleen Machut

Autumn leaves fell upon the ground,
Welcome winter. Gone are my words,
With the migration of the birds.
The glisten of a snow-topped mound;
A safe haven where hope is found.
Spring's arrival brings more goodbyes,
Replacing robin's lullabies.
Swiftly, the cycle of the moon,
Finds comfort in the cuckoo's tune.
No time to mourn winter's demise.

Birds and Seasons Décima
Rachael Holmes

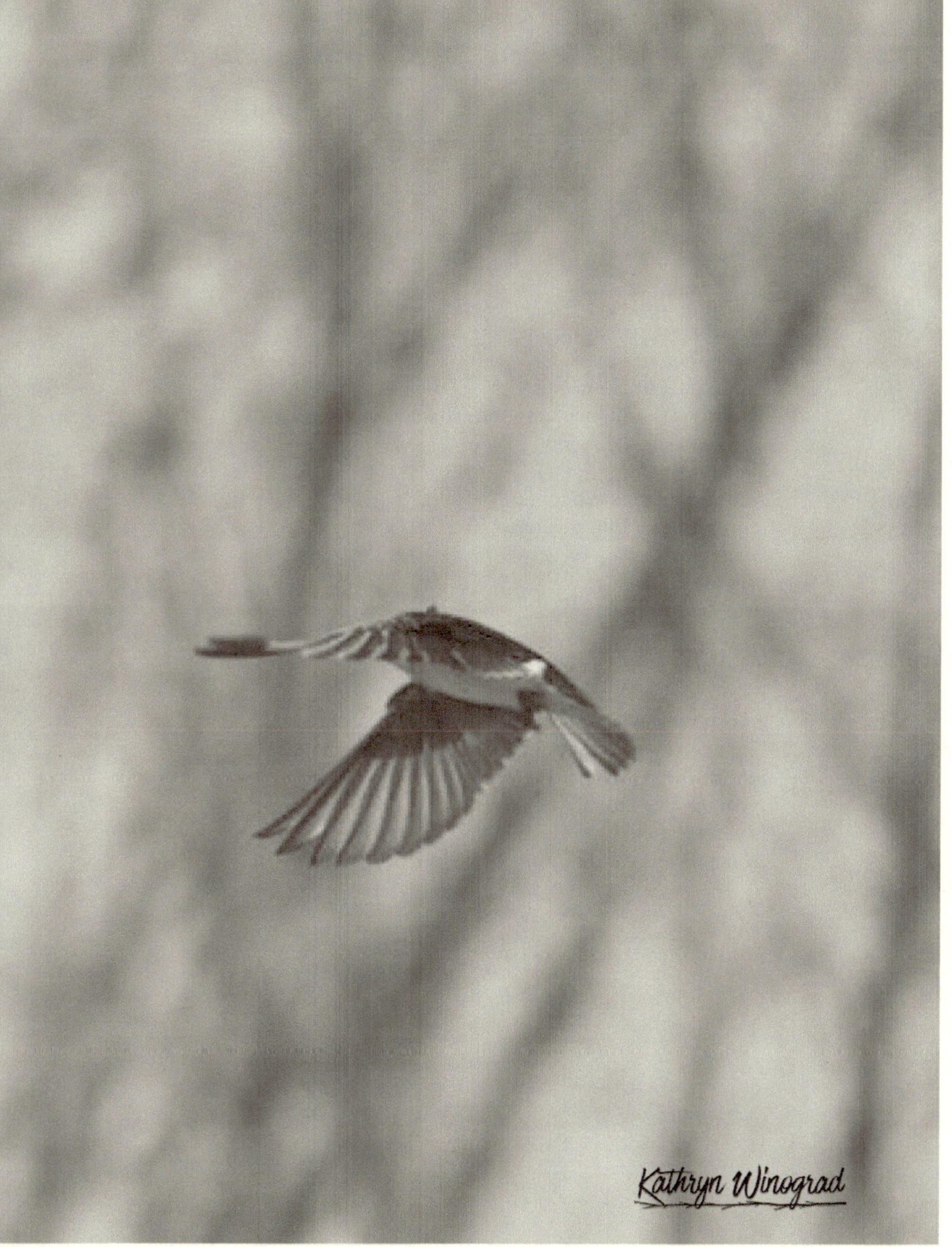
Kathryn Winograd

Rain drops spread my ink,
Thousands of verses,
Thousands of memories,
Thousands of hidden emotions that are mouthful,
The spinal cord like sky,
Sketch its pain,
And scribble it's thoughts,
Rain scribes it into our heart,
Shading under a tree,
Wet my clothes,
And damps the tar road,
How deep can the underground hear the rain's emotion?
Sudden chill and sadness,
Fills the heart,
As if it was soaked into a bucket of sad water,
How deep the roots can gasp the rain's emotion?
Floods the street,
Floats in our thought of past,
Muds the forest,
And showered the mountains of hurt.

Rain Drops
Jainisha Sadacharam

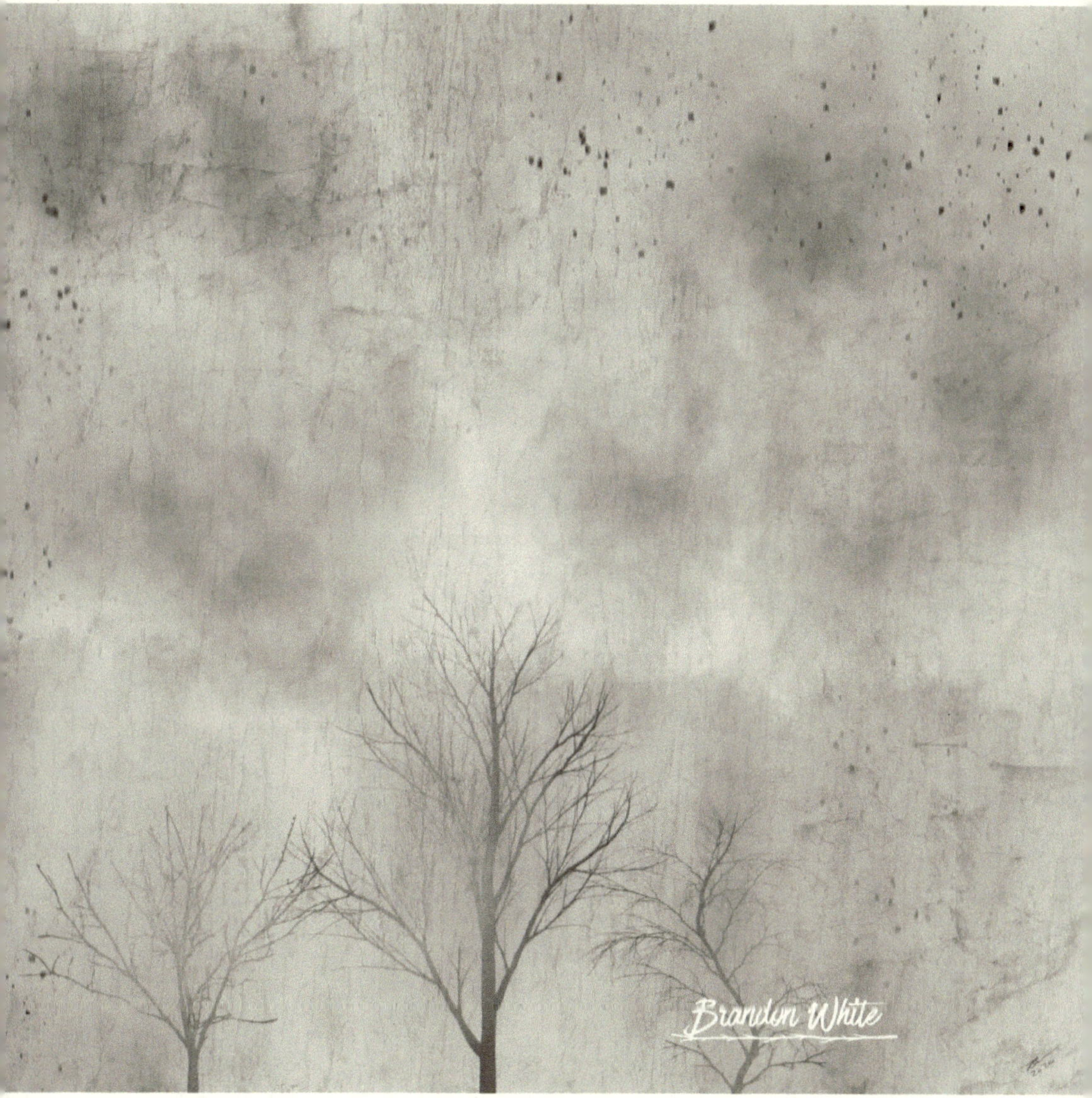

So little you know, wild-winged
and unshaken beneath a dog star,
half-grazing the pines, the bare winter
aspen I stand in the dark wash of
waiting for the tip of a yellow moon.
In Ohio, girlhood, these April stars
circled a pond bull-dozed
by my father, a raft of cattail
where the red-wings spun their nests
above the scrim of caught water.
Tonight, in this near dark, so close
my hand could circle it,
Sirius hovers above the red
factory lights of Pueblo
and the Sangre de Cristo blue-
washed in this hour.
I am cold in this wind,
in this spine of the Milky Way,
these blue white stars named
for a bear or a lyre or a woman
weeping her dead into a river.
I think I was still half-sleeping
in a field of grass, in a haze
of stars, in a far and nameless
country you care nothing
about, burying and unburying
those I love. Such quiet,
the mining trucks to the north
stalled and the little generator
of a shed where no one lives
in winter shut down.
And then, your wings, almost,
against the moon. Why
must we always be alone,
searching for something
beautiful?

To the Three Ducks Flying
Beneath the Dog Star
Kathryn Winograd

Scintillating, soaring seagulls
Scrambling sideways in the ocean to catch its prey
Searching silently on the shore for blankets filled with treats
Standing on one leg before me
Wondering who I am and posing for a portrait on a grain of sand
Lifting up in puffs of air towards a teal blue sky
Shadows against the clouds with armor like strands of wings and wild legs
Landing on a grey stone rock pretending to cliff dive onto the ridged
Landing
Dancing to the songs of the breeze
They lift together performing music, singing to each other
Scintillating, soaring seagulls

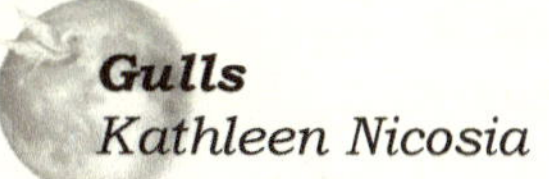

Gulls
Kathleen Nicosia

i understand
why flies
buzz
&
crash
into the glass
of your windows
desperate
to escape
the stale air
desperate
to feel
the breeze
on
their
wings.

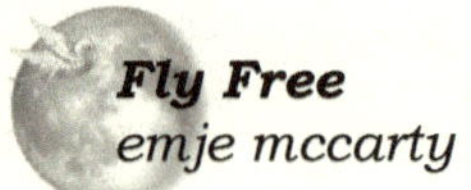

Fly Free
emje mccarty

Swifts crisscross
The late evening sky,
Its slate-grey clouds leaden
With the expectation of rain.
Their silhouette wings
Pierce the pregnant gloom,
Like arrows through
Love's aching hearts.
A Spring dance
Long and languorous
Weaves its tapestry
High above the eye
Which watches for a sign
A trail to leave a clue
To love's lost song
Of whispers on the breeze,
As silent still
They soar.

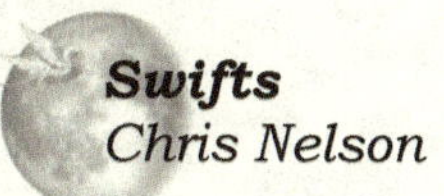

Wind and rain are a desert gift
It powers the windmills
that light up the earth
and channel the sacred

There are no illusions or mirages
to entice our imagination,
just windmills in the mist--
broad, white, and extending

Spinning in time and space,
stretching up through the rain,
into the face of the gray clouds
with the sun blinded by the fog.

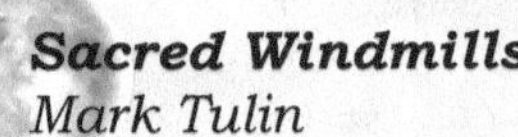

Sacred Windmills
Mark Tulin

Jimmi Campkin

Formless, we circle,
discs floating, hurricane clouds,
blusters of energy surging,
coursing through bloodless veins
around a neutral heart.

We spit out the extra,
heat release, entropy,
a search for rationality
in a world that refuses it,
refuses us peace of spinning minds.

Neither here nor there, up nor down,
but what is direction to us,
to cycles of movement beyond time,
beyond the creatures we inhabit,
parasites of life, necessary evils?

Without there is nothing,
and yet we too are nothing,
weightless, forever trapped
in cycles, irrationality
the only escape from normality.

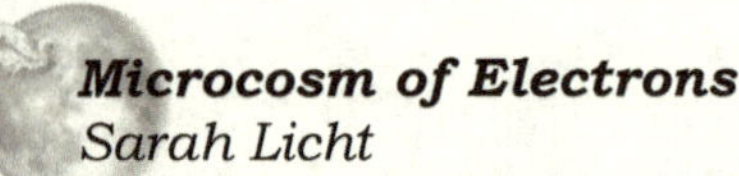

I am waiting for the starlings
to take me with them
They are past my perch so fast
I'm lost before found

wondering what I have missed
this time in their urgent work
going south going someplace
familiar I cannot go

I hear the last of the whoosh of wings
the sound of their mysteries
the weightlessness of their murmurs,
sky maps sung year after year

They crease the face of the wind
great rafts of kind, hungry in fall colors
disappearing into the sun, all that's left
of tiny brave hearts beating in mine.

If naked enough our wings might show and call us
to fly now, great rushing air and feathers boiling
shapeshifting dust of souls, pilots arriving
on winter grounds, folding wings, none left behind.

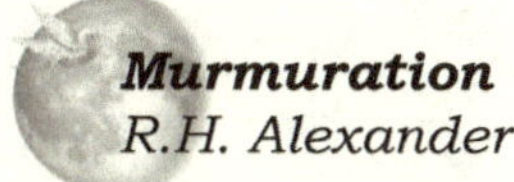

Murmuration
R.H. Alexander

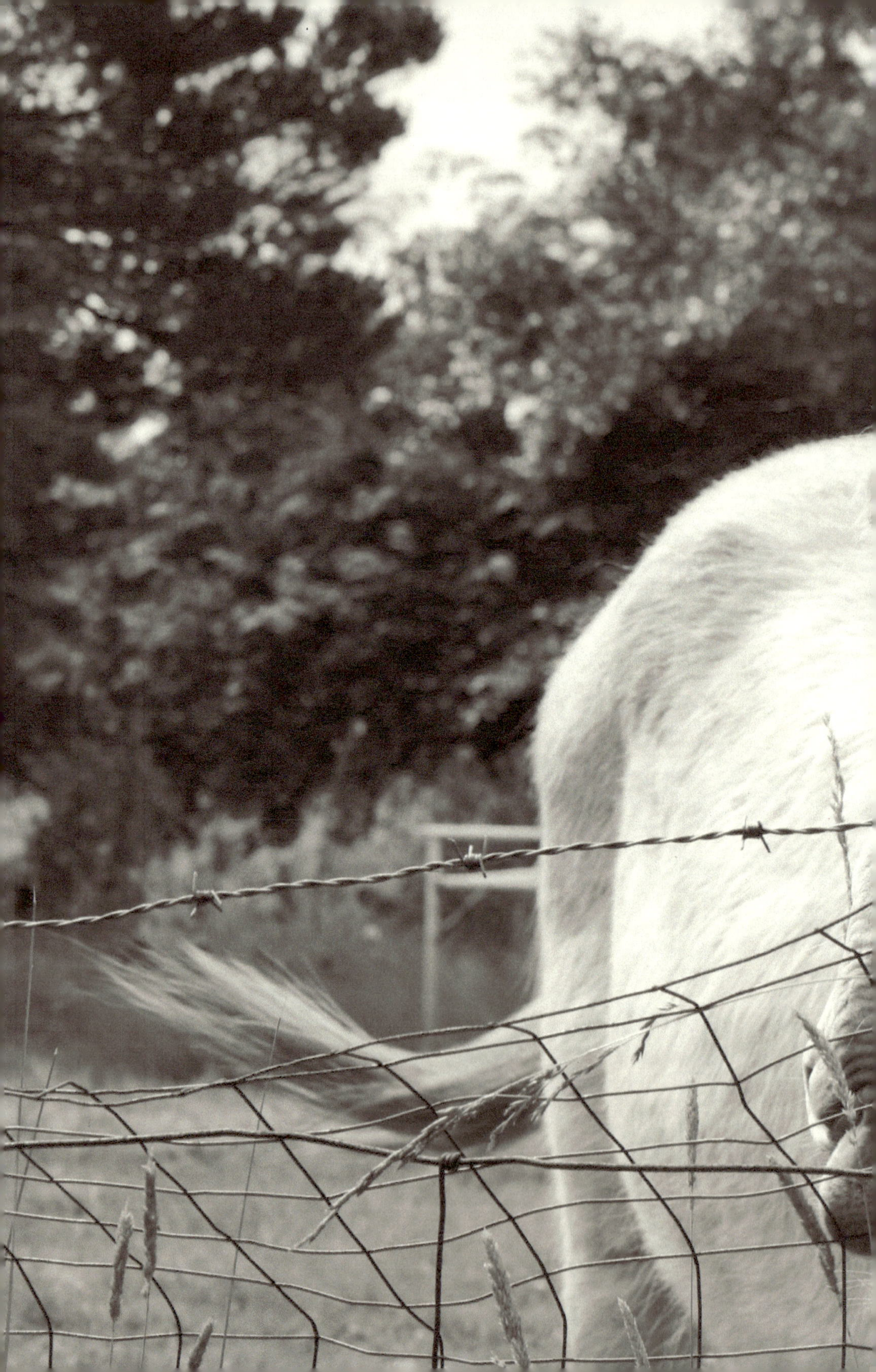

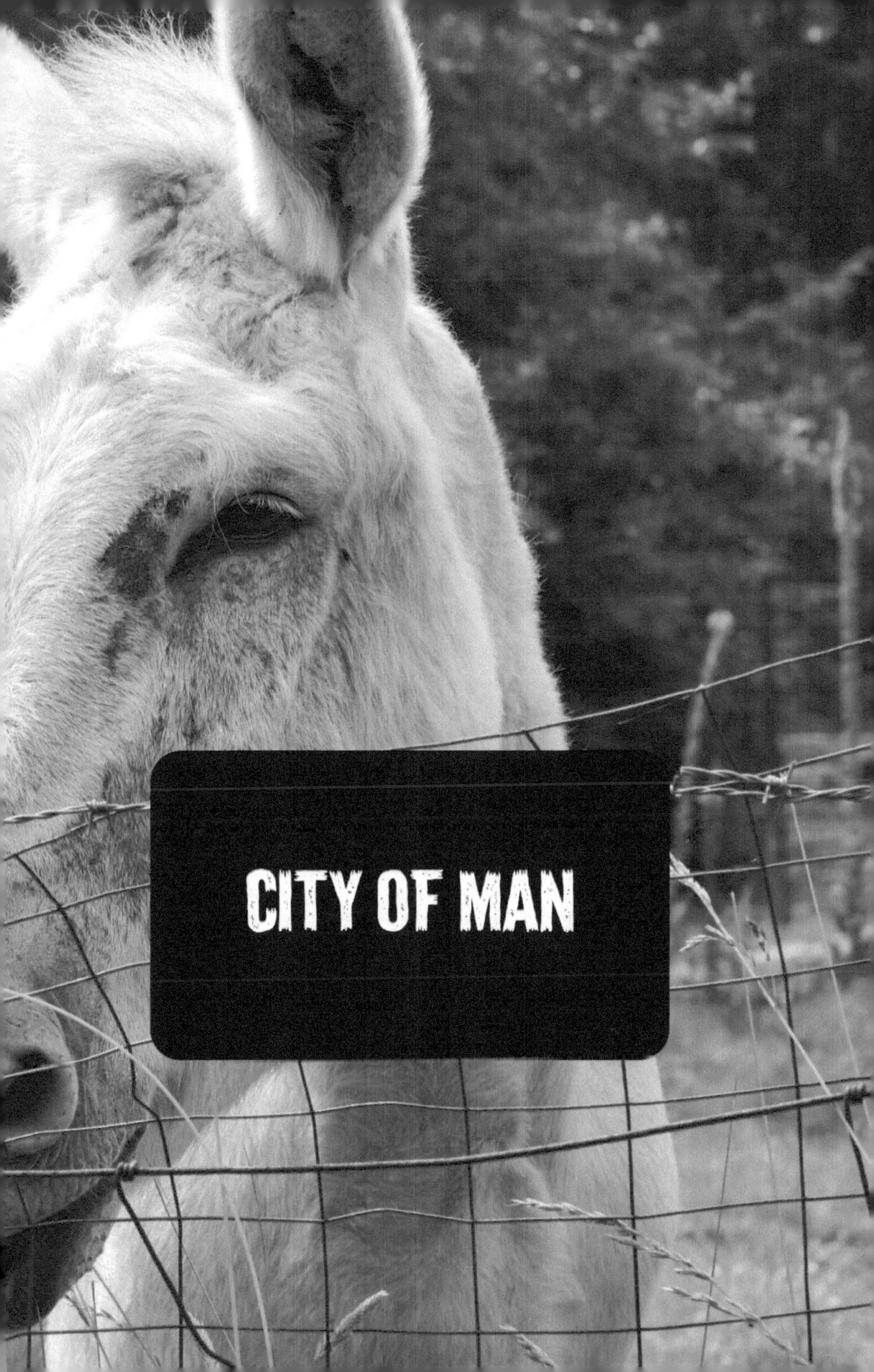
CITY OF MAN

I've fallen for your sacred treasures
Mesmerized by your everlasting glance
I've fallen for your marvelous touch
Captivated by your glowing center

Forever celebrating my life with you
Fallen for the glass ocean
Never will you break
Cradling your affection

I've fallen for your calm and luscious fields
Enamored by your wide eyed sensitivity
I've fallen for your irresistible smile
Fascinated by your precious sandcastles

Forever celebrating my life with you
Fallen for the glass ocean
Never will you break
Cradling your affection

I've fallen for your wildfire of a breeze
Enchanted by your celestial scent
I've fallen for your warm embrace
Enraptured by your brilliant skin

Forever celebrating my life with you
Fallen for the glass ocean
Never will you break
Cradling your affection

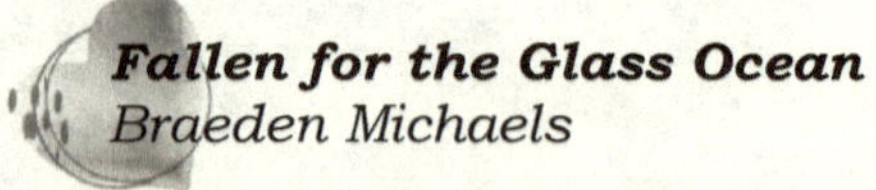

Fallen for the Glass Ocean
Braeden Michaels

She fell upon my hard cover
book on the lives of caterpillars
from a wispy cedar tree burl
I scared away an excited robin
and some boys with fishing poles
I watched her crawl back and forth
doing a 50 leg two step on my arm
She began to weave a golden chrysalis
forged in the loom of transformation
Someday soon she will emerge
unfettered in chaotic trajectories
Draped in winged coruscation
like an angelic stowaway
tucked safely inside
Buddha's hip pocket

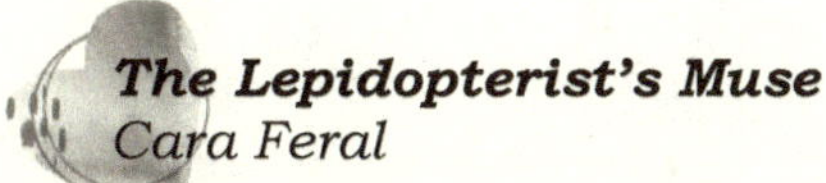
The Lepidopterist's Muse
Cara Feral

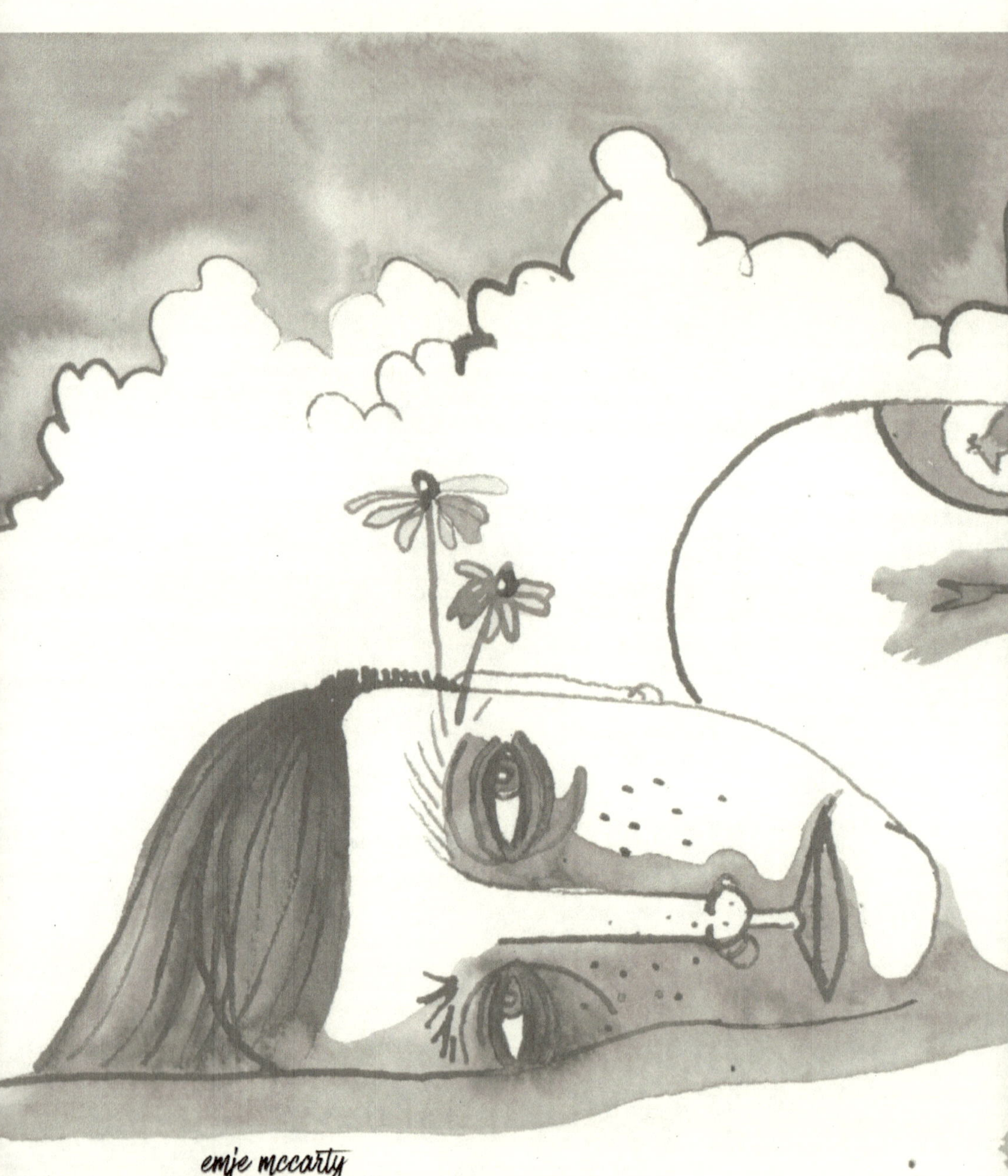

emje mccarty
'FOR ALL MY SCREAMING'

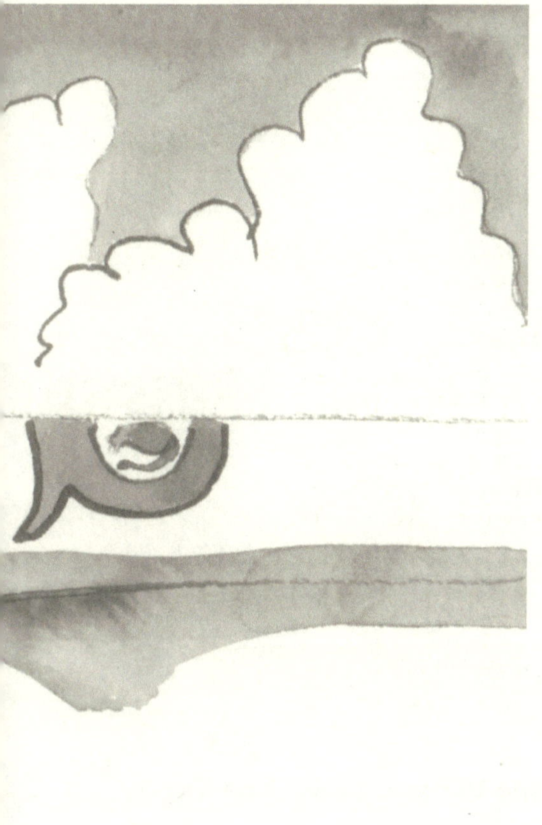

the weather today
it reminds me
of you
of you...& me
warm sun
& blue skies
quickly eclipsed
with bitter winds
& april snow
no...wait…
here comes the sun
&…
a sudden cloud
cover
with a frigid
blast
of spring snow
no...no...see…
it's sunny again
& all is well
...just don't look to the horizon
...not yet…
storm clouds!
no.
sunshine

Spring Snow Shower
emje mccarty

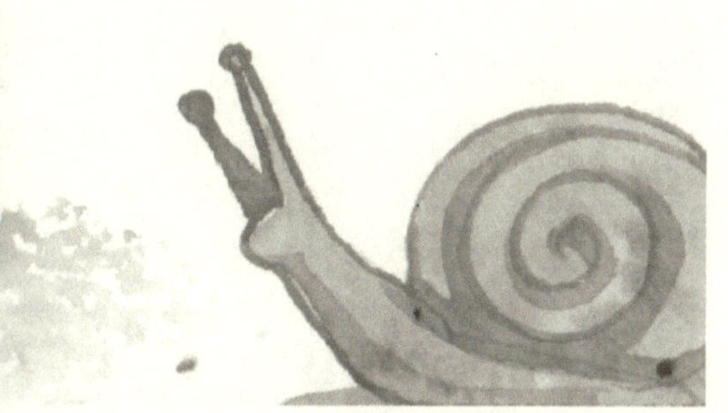

Foot on the fence post
Looking out on the land
The sky seems bluer these days
She told me she loved me
With her dying last breath
Seventeen years, today
Back when I was young and alive
Stars and dreams on the horizon
Me and Molly kept on without her
Sunsets never look the same
But today I heard her voice
In the western wind
And I know my time's near done
Molly's got her own baby now
All this would always be hers
I'll be coming soon, my Agatha dear
And the blue sky will be even bluer

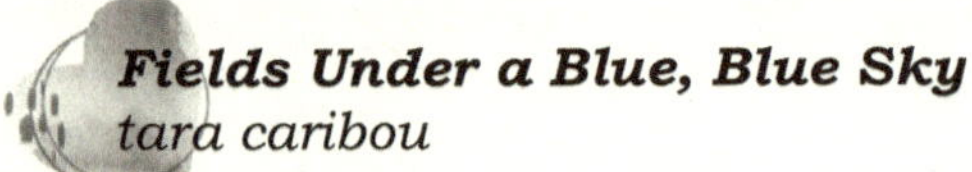

Fields Under a Blue, Blue Sky
tara caribou

In the extremities of that departure.
Where the ground gave way and the stars beckoned.
In the evidence of brilliance.
That wandering elation into nothingness.
Searching for a home, some place to land.
I take down that crucified past.
Bury it in the soil that is now beneath my feet.
Sweet sand that follows in my shoes.
As the earth hums a hot vibration.
Not returned.
Not remained.
Yet back again to where I find it.
Wiping the turmoil from this skin.
Swallowing sanity for the first time.
Breathing that eucalyptus air that floods and scares me.
Missing nothing, but tomorrow.

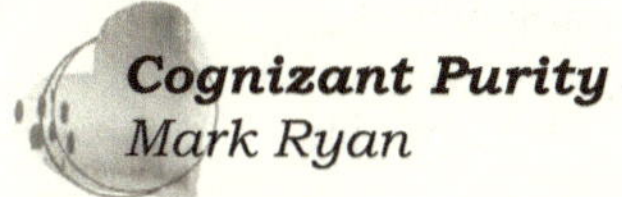

A forest blooms before us,
ashen spring petals dropping,
a shower of pinks and reds
to match the color in our cheeks,
speckled heat like the sun above
blazing the trees to summer flame.

Stars breath life, flames coursing,
a dance for two beneath the thicket
of ample oak trees high above,
the world green and pure under feet
unsteady on earth cracked, dehydrated
yet continuing on ad infinitum.

Hearty leaves change with us,
change colors like the rising sun,
frail, fragile to touch, a forest
without the mercy of heat, preparing
for the bitter cold to strip it from love,
us from flowers soggy with autumnal rain.

A forest bleeds before us,
branches dripping icicles, coagulating
needles clinging to bare feet,
motionless against the frost
yet waiting for the sun to rise again,
to see if we bloom too like rosy petals.

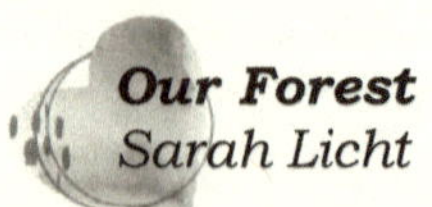

Our Forest
Sarah Licht

tara caribou

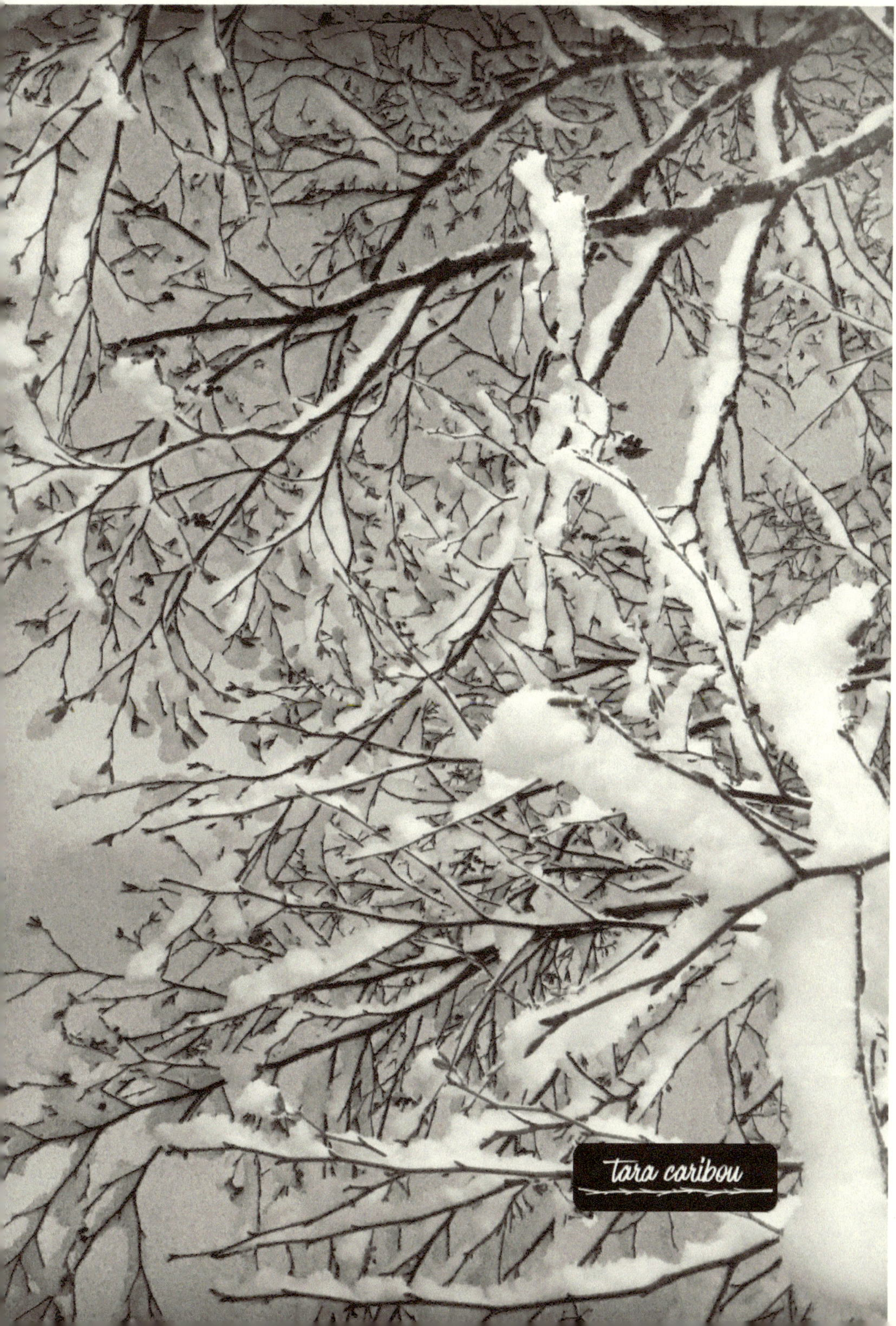

This vast expanse of emptiness, hollowed out by heavenly hands
A powder blue dream just out of reach
We are children of earth and clay
Yet we have always longed for the sky

An artist's muse, an inventor's wildest dream
We traced our wing bones for wings
And built our own when we found none

This ancient entity which surrounds us all
We were once a part of it
Dust to ashes, ashes to dust

To be weightless and free and unbound
To feel the unrestrained fury of it all
A speck in that heavenly canvas of smears and rolling hues
Where clouds would curl around our unrelenting forms

We are weary beings, grounded and rooted and bound here
Yet we chase the biting kiss of the wind, fill our lungs to the point of spilling
And dream and dream and dream

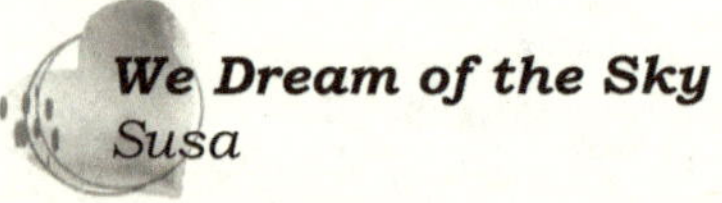

these days
treading water is a victory;

at least I'm breathing.

at least
I can feel the air
and sun, rain, wind on my face.

if I'm really lucky I float for a while
catching my breath and resting
my arms in a lull in the waves.

some days I inhale deeply
and dive down to the ocean floor
in search of some smooth and shiny
iridescent treasure;

cupping it in my palm, I swim
back up to the surface;

uncurl my fingers
eager to share it with anyone
who's close enough to see
and alive enough to care.

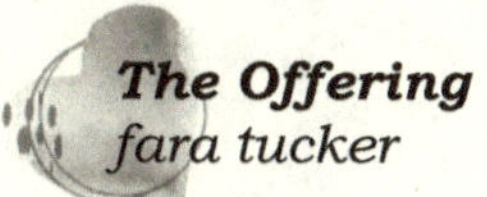

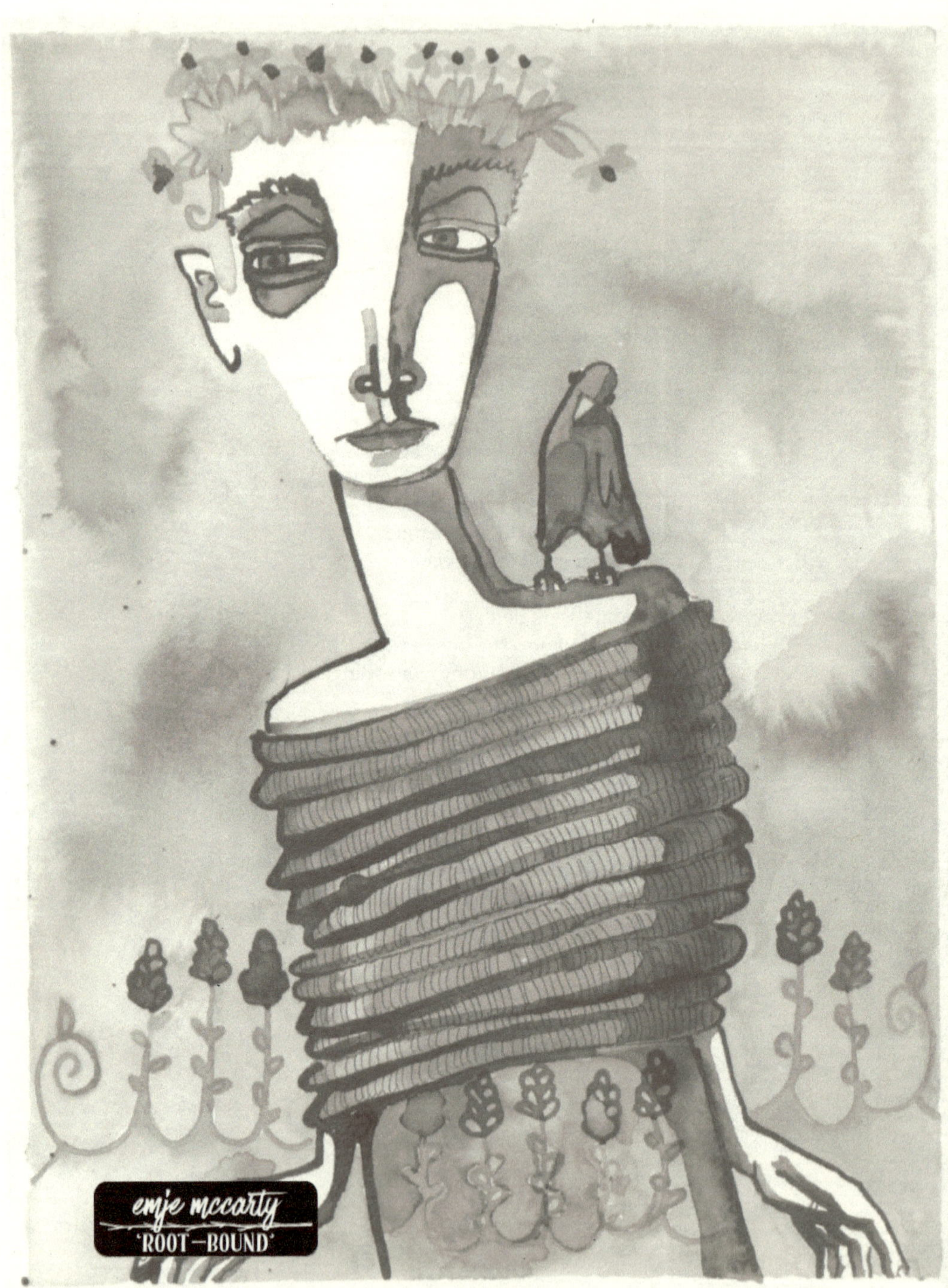
emje mccarty
'ROOT—BOUND'

Sackman, lives up on the mountain
throwing off the shackles of mainstream life
drinking from the streams and bathing in the rains
eating bread from heaven baked over rocks.

Sackman, lives up on the mountain
living off its bounty is all he craves
down in the city trading and persuading
selling roots and remedies made the ancient way.

Sackman, who d'you think you're kidding?
Who's going to save you from city life
Call upon your gods, call upon your heritage
nothing's going to save you from the modern world.

Sackman on the Mountain
Chris Hall

And the nightfall drips a callous venom
A sour chill crawls until the dawn cracks
Separation of anguish and stillness
Filled with distinctions and extinctions
Exasperated colors disappear in the mist
The Bloodhound river relinquishes agony
Hurricanes chained to a dreary atmosphere
And the October sun cries

I walk with sympathy in the clouds
I run with ignorance in my pockets
I discarded the truth like a pile of dirt
Goodbye to the sunlight

And the somber morning is torn and frayed
A harsh thunder awakens the disturbance
Dissolution of uncertainty and empty shrieks
Wrapped up in sinister winds and anger
Distressed shades appear in the haze
The oceans of reclusion surrender
Catastrophes grumble in the glare
And the October sun cries

I with sympathy in the clouds
I run with ignorance in my pockets
I discarded the truth like a pile of dirt
Goodbye to the sunlight

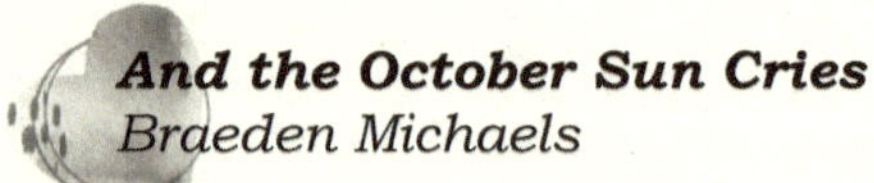

You are mouthfuls of rain
and eyes of rolling thunder,
snowcapped emotions and
she-loves-me-not conundrums.

And I am feverish remorse
and avalanches of white flags turning red
under sarsaparilla skies.

I'd place dreams on the tails of comets
and leave atmospheric burns across your skin
if only we could travel
to a time before the fireflies escaped and
we trapped lightning in bottles.

Perhaps then you can suture the pieces of me
that are no longer me and
the fragments of you that separates our flesh
from bone and love from lust
and cauterize truth and hope back together.

Perhaps then we will collapse breathless and shaking,
bare and breaking at Eros' altar
and claim a heart that beats
to the rhythm of forgotten fables.

Perhaps then, with a steady hand
and haunted heart
I will chop love's martyrdom off at the knees
so it can no longer run.

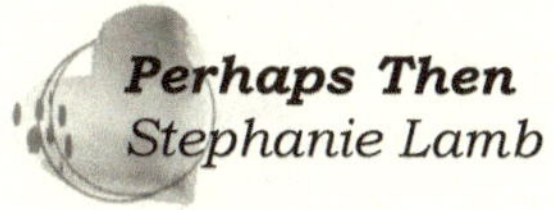

Perhaps Then
Stephanie Lamb

The sky, not even bruised,
spills its light, blue
as the petals of the wild iris
wound in their buried boats
beneath the morning fire
ash I throw to the cold
wind, again. I think
the iris, named for a rainbow
goddess of such purity
and loved so by a god,
must belong to early
summer, and so it will not
rise yellow-eyed and soon
in my dark harbors of grass
and aspen root no matter
what I dreamed last night
or who I wept for
or how long I linger in this gold
slip of sun on the porch step.
Maybe tomorrow, in tiny
pockets of earth and worn
granite or in this last snow
that does not drift away,
I will find the pasque-flower.
And quiet and trembling for its
purpled flesh and early
blossom, I will call
it love, and sorrow, too.

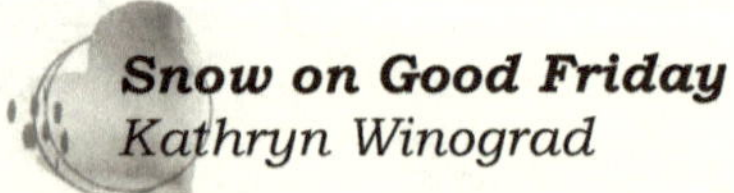

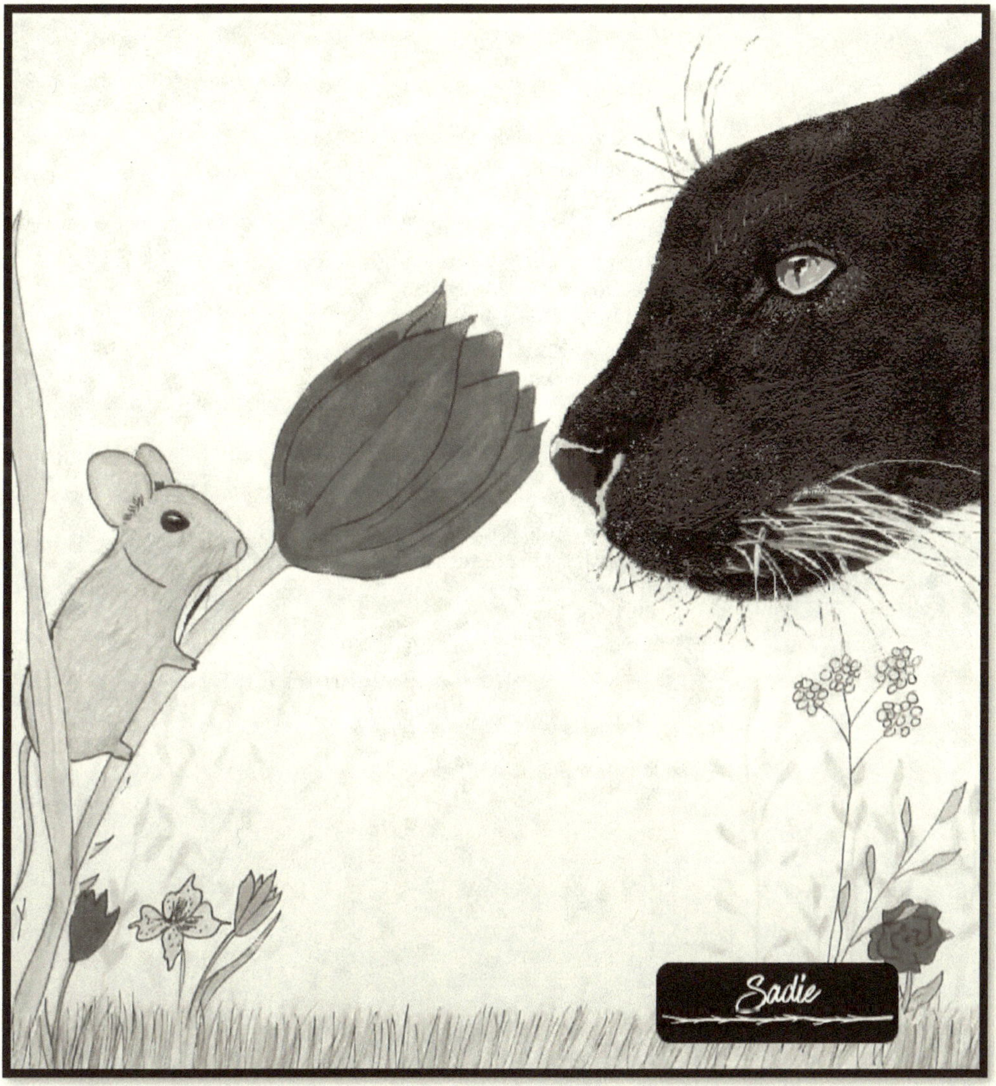

Sadie

He shouts "rocku" at stones
in yards and parks,
Caws at the crows,
and points to roses.
He throws the ball to a dog,
tries to eat the fence,
and buries his fingers
in the warm infield dirt.
He greets waves at beaches,
pushes on pepper trees,
observes turtles observing him,
and beams at the sky.
He's a baby and he sees,
without interrupting,
the spring breeze move
all the leaves at once.

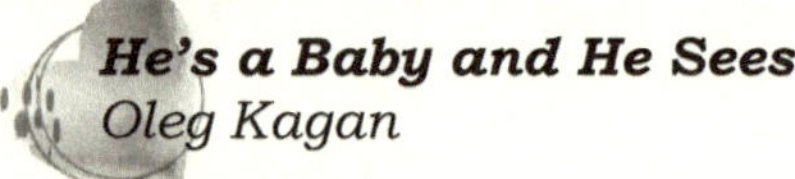
He's a Baby and He Sees
Oleg Kagan

a reluctant
moon
veiled in the shadows
of the past
struggling to rise
past the horizon
tendrils
unfurling
flower moon
if only i can climb
higher
into the sky
to see past
my worries
& shine brightly
for all
to see.

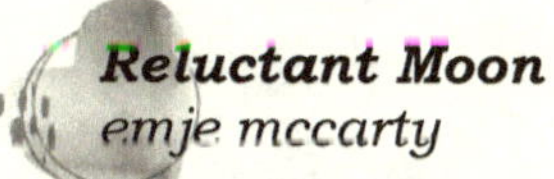

Reluctant Moon
emje mccarty

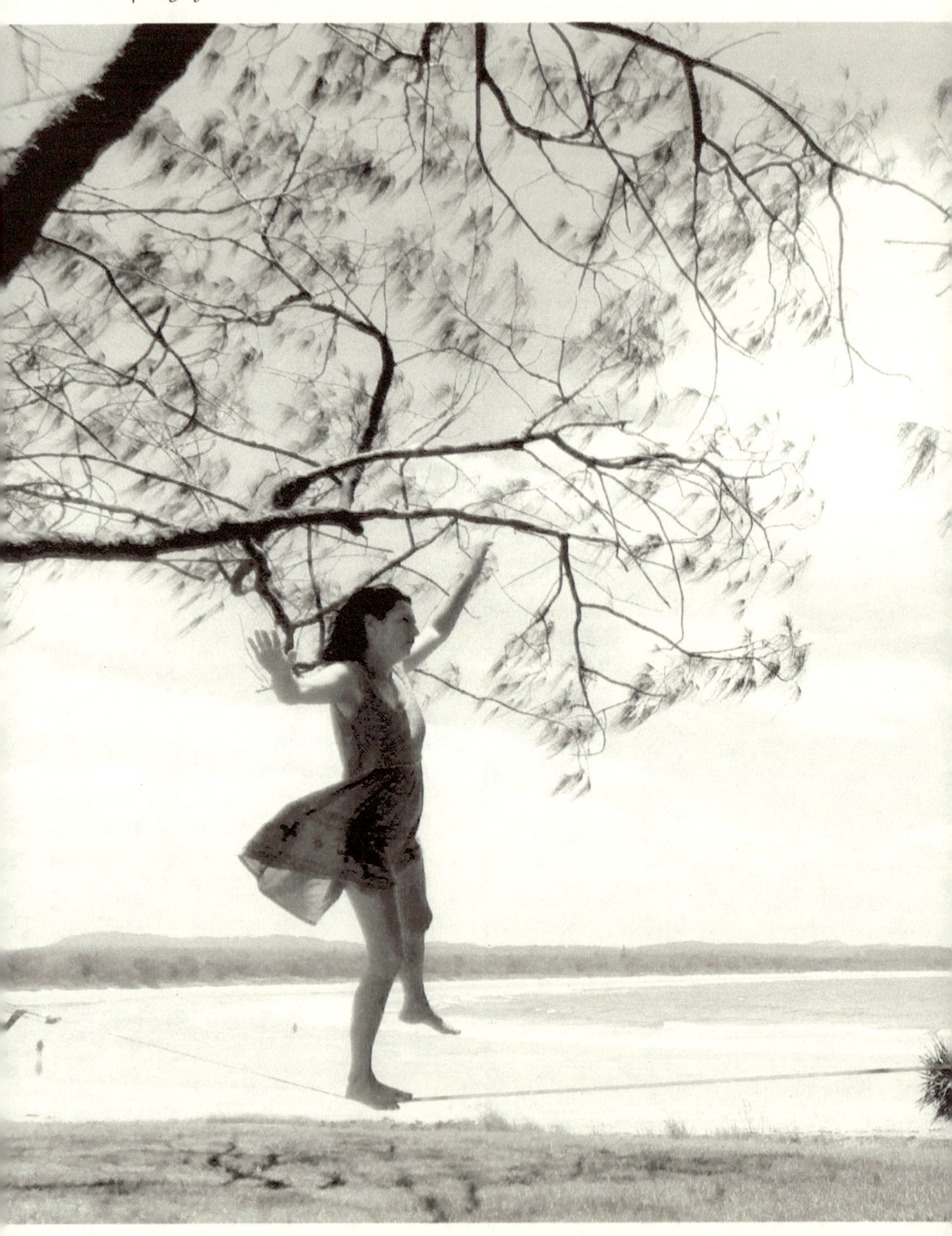

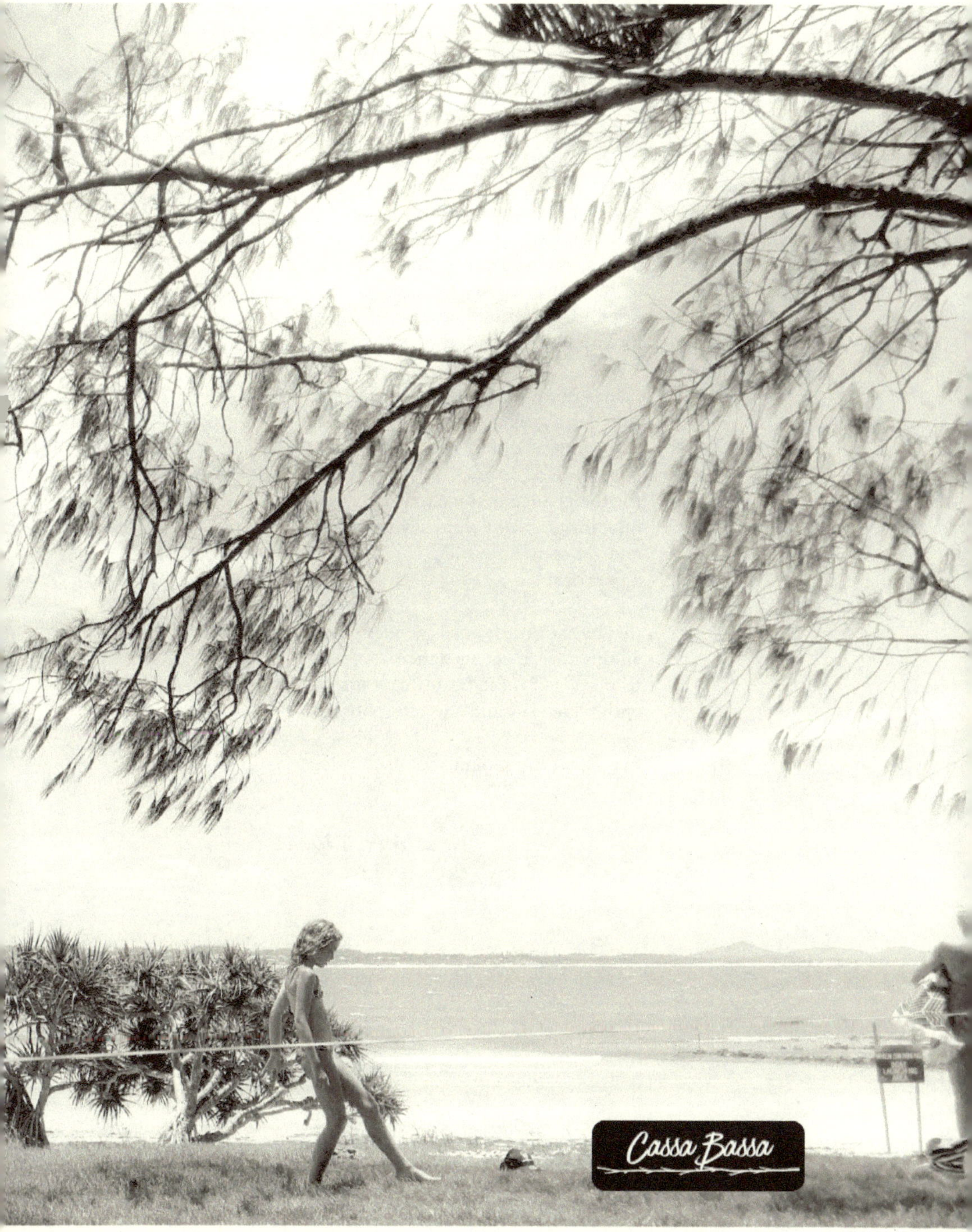

driven by science or beauty
to stare into the sky;
hopeful, shivering humans
lookup in anticipation of awe.

planes upon planes upon boats;
shlepping gear
and cautious optimism;

for the chance that we may be reminded
how insignificant we really are
and yet somehow still
a part of it all.

maybe the Aurora has traveled
all this way to see us dance--
to marvel at these beautiful souls
with wide eyes and shivering bodies.

maybe we are looking for each other.

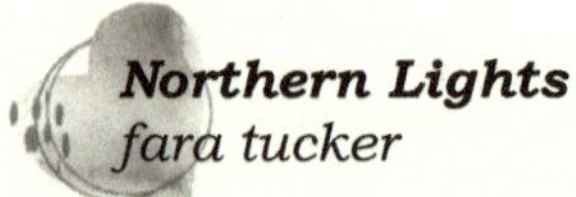

Northern Lights
fara tucker

beneath our tree
where my lungs come back to me
for it is there
among borrowed ears
the cadence of you, of i
falls freely
beneath blooming arms,
those towering magic wands
those leaves, an artistic blend of hues
lent by the color of our words
birthed from our woes, our joys
now drip dropping in tiny doses
a repertoire of moments
gifts caressed from our swollen lips
beneath this our found sanctum
a secret place, a perfect hiding spot
where treasured scribing
and whispers in the wind
hold a love affair in soft reverie
infused within the veins of its hollow
beyond distances they traveled
weathered testaments of time
reaching for the sun
how they glow
how it flows
upwards
outwards
reflecting within
beneath our tree
where my lungs come back to me

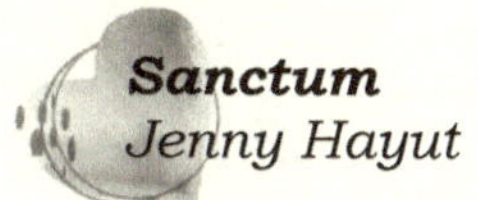
Sanctum
Jenny Hayut

Is the river wrong
to smooth the stones?
Is the wind a tyrant
for humbling crags?

Year after eon,
nature wields its easy power,
patiently shaping itself --
a slow violence,
while we,
pugilists of existence,
flail authority like a chain-mace,
gashing others and ourselves.

We bearers of pocket knives,
carve our short-lived names
into bamboo shoots,
as if that
makes them ours.

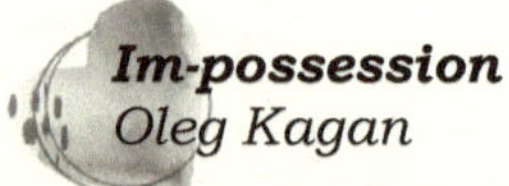

Im-possession
Oleg Kagan

Blood drizzles
a puzzle, wends
through these woods

sprays the duff
giving, hinting~
red leaves ahead.

Hope flows but in
drops and specks.
Brushstrokes, rain, tears.

Everything is blood
nothing is blood, panic
is blood I can't see.

Ahead a deer lies still,
impatient. No more
flicking ears or running.

For the chance to pray
for its burst heart
for the heat that will rise

thanks are given.
For this wild gift, I bow.
I am sorry to take its life.

But I have seen
its spirit rise again
in the strength

of my children
and their children.
In their vivid eyes wide open

around my table
into the world,
Amen.

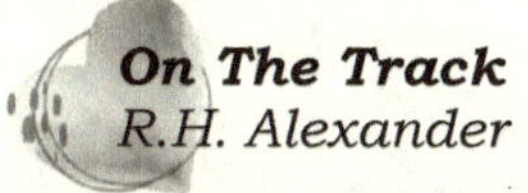

On The Track
R.H. Alexander

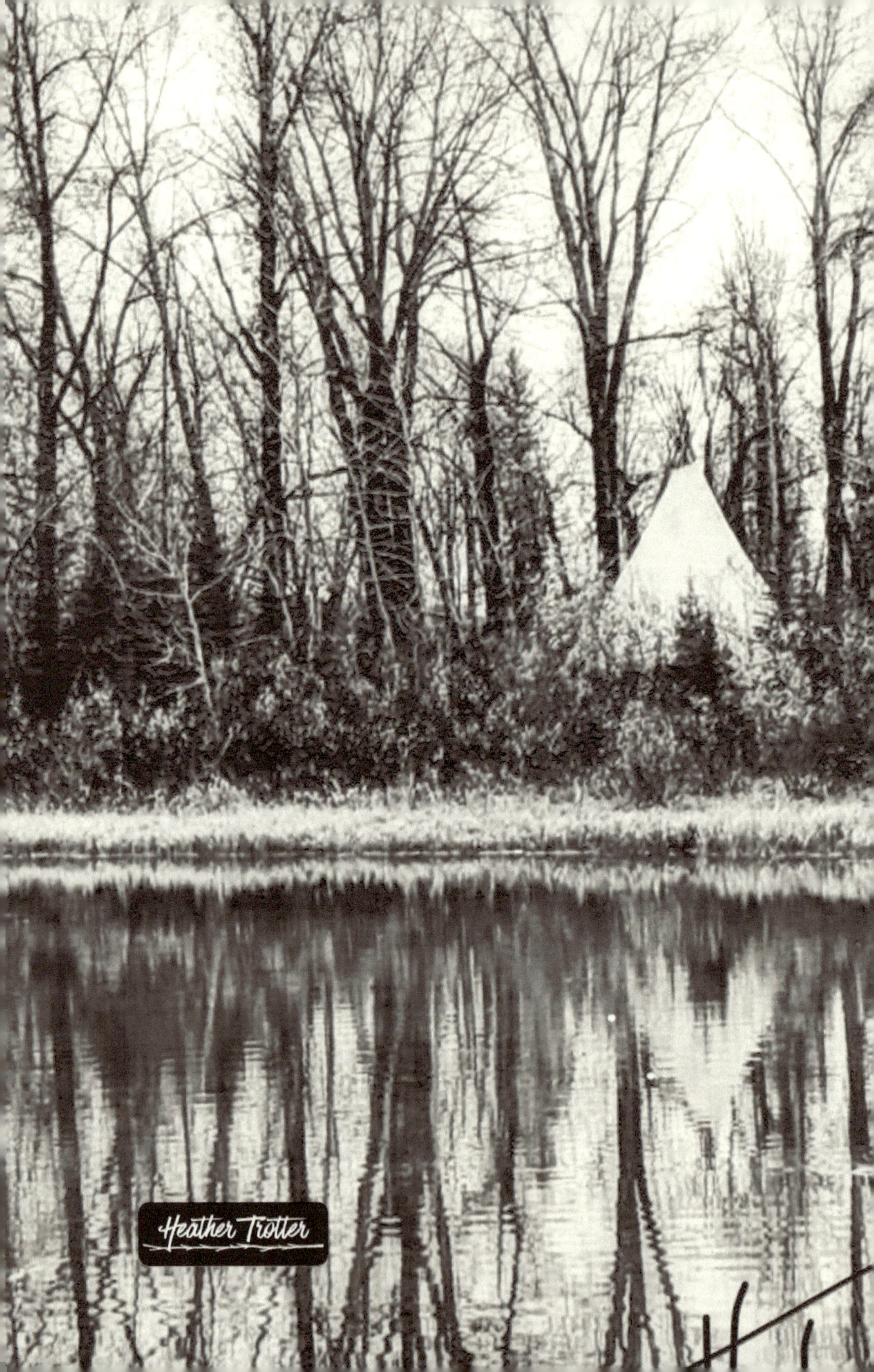
Heather Trotter

It has gone cold all of the sudden
It's inevitable to notice
You have arrived
My fingers are cold when touching my lukewarm lips

I close my eyes recollecting your splendid beauty
The rain sprinkling on my lashes
When the chill air seeping through my poncho
The scarf and beanie keeping me genial
Hiking boots springing on soggy ground layed with unspoken words from dreams last night
I see those lost words in colours sage, forest, bumblebee, pumpkin, crimson, scarlet...

Taking a deep breath in, looking up
You're opening up to me like a peacock in a palette of fall
Except, you gravitating to the earth easing off my anxious mind
Allowing me to taste and digest every inch of your abundant glory

Time is far from the essence

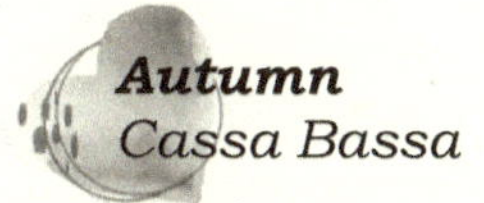

Tempests swell and test the land
Waves collapsing with concussive force
Winds tearing sails and flooding yachts
The walls pressured and buckle
The harbor seeking shelter on land
Throw money into the storm in futility
Shelter ripped away in an instant
The water filling your bedroom to your knees
Boats flurry through city streets

Fires rage against the city
Lightening cries for war and the fields answer
Dry and brown left to sway in the waves of heat
Wildlife fleeing in all directions
The flames hunger insatiable
Leaves, grass, homes, and mountain sides
It all burns and we catch ash fall

Earth resisting its own vacancy
Shuttering at the loss
Grief manifest in water and fire
May we mourn extinction

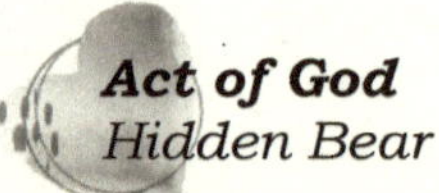

I reflect on the time we met
on the edge of the stars.

We danced our way along the milky way,
landing softly on the red sandy dunes of Mars.

Just on the edge of forever
and the brink of something new.

We watched andromeda disappear into a black hole and
reappear in another dimension ten times as bold.

Lotus flowers bloomed from my palms
and roots sprouted from my feet.

And for those brief seconds I was free
from the hurricane brewing inside of me.

And I could hear the hands of time
marching in reverse.

I was met with the memory of us
in the curvature of my mind and
for a few blissful moments,
all of time and space, *and even we*,
belonged to the stars.

I had never been closer to nirvana
than when Mars was ours.

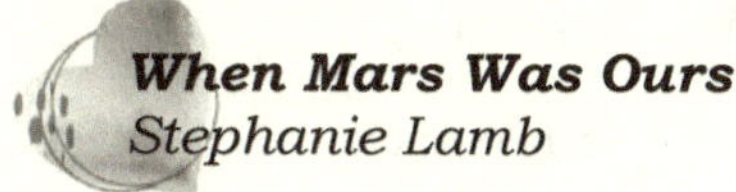

When Mars Was Ours
Stephanie Lamb

Index of Artists

Index of Artists, Cont'd

Contributor Biographies

BRAEDEN MICHAELS is an American author and creator of Deconstructive Literature. He has been published in *Static Dreams Volume One* and *The Poets Symphony*. He has released six poetry books including *The Raven's Poison* and *Stella Walker's Acquaintances*, available on all major retailers. He continues his journey as a writer.

Blog: Storm of Ink at *braedenmichaels.com*
Instagram: *@braeden_michaels_author*

BRANDON WHITE is a poet, songwriter, proud husband, and father of twins from Fort Smith, Arkansas. He has released multiple EPs and albums (all available on your favorite streaming service). White's work has appeared in several anthologies and has three poetry collections to date, *The Year that Stole the Light Away*, *Real Big American Zen,* and *A Boat for the Sinking*, available at major retailers.

Blog: *brandonwhitemusicandpoetry.com*
Instagram: *@brandonwhitemusicandpoetry*
Goodreads: *goodreads.com/ brandonwhitemusicandpoetry*

CARA FERAL is from the high plains of Laramie, Wyoming. She earned a physics degree in Kutztown University. She later dropped out of a full ride scholarship to study astrophysics at Louisiana State University to go hike the Appalachian Trail. Since then, she has thru-hiked the Appalachian Trail two times, the 2,600-mile Pacific Crest Trail, and the 3,300-mile Continental Divide Trail. Eventually she wants to be the first trans-woman to complete the quadruple crown by hiking the 4,600-mile North Country Trail. These days she quarantines inside the cozy confines of her apartment with her cat and boyfriend in Eugene, Oregon.

Blog: *thetigressawakes.wordpress.com*
Twitter: *@cara_feral*

CASSA BASSA China-born Australian poet Jia-Li (Cassa Bassa) works with the disadvantaged people in the community which gives her a special insight into those that suffer. She is constantly inspired by their resilience and strength. An inquisitive writer that was a bit of a misfit as a child, she has blossomed into her writing. Jia-Li's poetry has been published in the Australian Poetry Journal Volume 8 and *The Poets Symphony* from Raw Earth Ink. Her debut collection of micro-fiction *The Scars We Don't See* is available at major retailers. Read more on her blog.

Blog: *flickerofthoughts.com*
Instagram: *@cassa_bassa*

CG TENPENNY is a poet, singer/songwriter, and photographer.

Blog: *moltenpoetry.com*
Instagram: *@moltenpoetry*

CHRIS HALL describes herself as compulsive story teller, cat slave and hen keeper, who lives in the Western Cape of South Africa. So far she has published three novels and a collection of short stories. Her work was included in *Writing My City,* an anthology published for the 2019 Open Book Festival in Cape Town.

Blog: *lunasonline.wordpress.com*
Instagram: *@chris_hall_author_pics*
Goodreads: *goodreads.com/chris_hall*

CHRIS NELSON was born in East Anglia, but grew up in Birmingham when his family relocated while he was still a young child. After leaving school, he studied computing at what was then Wolverhampton Polytechnic, before deciding that it was not a career path he wanted to follow. He retrained as a teacher and has taught in a primary school in Dudley since the mid-1980s. He has dabbled in writing short stories since his youth, but has begun writing more seriously since the turn of the century. His poetry appears in *The Poets Symphony* and his short story "The Guest House" in the collection *Static Dreams Volume Two.* Both publications are available through all good online outlets. He lives in Stourbridge with his wife and two children.

Blog: *chrisnelson61.wordpress.com*

COLLEEN MACHUT lives along the lake shore in Wisconsin with her husband Trent and son Desmond.

Website: *liveforever-project.org*

DONNA NONGKHLAW is an Assistant Audit Officer by profession at the Indian Audit and Accounts Department (IA&AD). Never in her wildest dreams did she ever envision herself writing poems; it came to her, nevertheless, like a hurricane. Though astounded, she is embracing it with both hands in limitless wonder.

DVON BRIDGEFORTH is 22 years old and was born and raised in Baltimore, Maryland by his mother and has two sisters and one brother. He began writing around the age of 11 when he realized he would grow up mostly alone without any siblings around. He was a pretty lonely kid so it was a way for him to pass the time. Dvon enjoyed reading, so that helped him understand English better since Spanish was his first language. His favorite activities are going to the gym, fishing, drawing, and playing the alto saxophone. Generally a quiet person, he isn't afraid to socialize but would rather be seen than heard in most cases due to severe trust issues. As a pagan, he is open to all people regardless of personal views or orientation.

Instagram: *@Valravyn_Odinson*

EMJE MCCARTY inks with bamboo pens and brushes. She likes to experiment with writing and inking graphic novels. Emje journals almost daily. She has published a book of neurotic comics and has a collection of self-portraits titled "the invisible exhibitionist" which is showing in the driftless region of Wisconsin where she lives and raises a horde of anarchists.

Blog: *emjemccarty.com*
Goodreads: *goodreads.com/ emjemccarty*

FARA TUCKER is a writer, poet, storyteller, teacher, photographer, former therapist and current therapy client. Originally from Brooklyn, New York, she's called Portland, Oregon home since 2000. Her poetry can be found in Train River Publishing's Spring 2020 Anthology and in the Summer 2020 of *Subjectiv.* – a journal of visual and literary art from the Pacific Northwest. She particularly loves exploring the beauty, heartbreak, and paradoxical nature of life and all its luminal spaces.

Blog: *faratucker.com*
Instagram: *@faratucker*

HEATHER TROTTER is a visual artist who enjoys drawing, painting, and photography. Her painting style is a unique blend of contemporary and pop-art. Drawing portraits of expressive characters is of keen interest. Spending time outdoors capturing inspiration while exploring urban and natural landscapes with her dog is a favorite pastime. She is drawn to reflections and the play of light casting shadows. She specializes in creating nostalgic art through commemorative custom projects.

Instagram: *@heathertrotterart*

HIDDEN BEAR is a Mechoopda poet and author originally from Northern California but currently living in North Carolina. He currently publishes his work on his website with writings about his life and his experience reclaiming the culture of his tribe. Growing up without his traditional culture has been painful but his is using poetry to connect to the culture, art, and spirit of his people. He has published two poetry collections *Moleskine on a coffee table* and *Suburb'n ndn* and was featured in *The Poets Symphony* from Raw Earth Ink.

Blog: *hiddenbearpoet.com*
Instagram: *@hiddenbearpoet*

JENNY HAYUT lives in Virginia with her family that includes her shelter rescue Georgia, an extremely spoiled beagle mix. Her love of writing began when she was twelve when she was introduced to haiku poetry and then later discovering and falling in love with the macabre master, Edgar Allan Poe. She describes her poetry as finding its inspiration by way of Poe and the romanticism found in the era of the Bronte sisters. She currently has three poetry books published as well as a romance series and has had work included in several online literary journals and anthologies.

Blog: *jennyhayut.org*
Instagram: *@JennyHayut*

JIMMI CAMPKIN is a writer and photographer currently living in the North East of England.

Website: *jimmicampkinphotography.com*
Blog: *jimmicampkin.com*
Instagram: *@jcampkinphoto*

JNC MAUVE is a persona she created for her readers, so it is her pen name. She has been writing poetry for the last five years. Her lifetime dream is to be known as a poet and a language practitioner. She is also the creator of *365 emotions* e-magazine. She wishes to die, leaving a prodigious amount of love for poetry.

Blog: *topdrawerortopbanana.blogspot.com*

KATHLEEN NICOSIA resides in Rocky Point, Long Island with her husband and her sweet cats Pearl and Ziggy. She is a retired school social worker who earned a BA in English and a Masters in Social work. She participates in a women's writing group called "The Woman's Way." She enjoys writing poetry, memoir, tap dancing, and singing.

KATHRYN WINOGRAD, *Writer@9600ft*, writes poetry and essays from her beloved cabin above Phantom Canyon in Colorado. A longtime educator and arts advocate, she is the author of six books and a winner of the Colorado Book Award in Poetry.

Blog: *kathrynwinograd.com*
Instagram: *@kathywinogra*
Goodreads: *goodreads.com/Kathryn_Winograd*

MARK RYAN was born in Oxford, growing up in the shadow of the dreaming spires. He studied film at London Metropolitan University, graduating to M.A in Film Theory. His work leans, bends, and sways to the metaphysical and supernatural, with a tendency to dabble in the macabre.

Website: *markryanhavoc.com*
Twitter: *@MarkRyan8289*
Goodreads: *goodreads.com/Mark_Ryan*

MARK TULIN's books include *Magical Yogis, Awkward Grace, The Asthmatic Kid and Other Stories*. His poems have appeared in *Amethyst Review, Strands Publishers, Fiction on the Web, Terror House Magazine, Beatnik Cowboy, Ariel Chart, Dreams in Fiction, Still Point Journal, the Writing Disorder*, and others. Mark is a retired psychotherapist who lives in Ventura, California with his wife, Alice.

Blog: *crowonthewire.com*
Instagram: *@ Crowonthewire_poetry*
Twitter: *@Crow_writer*

MEREDITH HELLER is a poet, singer/songwriter, and educator. A California poet in the schools, she teaches poetry workshops at Juvenile Hall and on Zoom for kids and adults. She is author of the poetry chapbook, *Songlines* (Finishing Line Press) and her new book, *Write a Poem, Save Your Life* (New World Library) published in spring of 2021. She is mused by nature, synchronicity, and kindred souls.

Blog: *BonesofSynchronicity.com*

OLEG KAGAN is an author, editor, speaker, writing coach, and librarian. He has had his writing published on sites all over the web, as well as numerous literary journals and anthologies.

Blog: *olegkagan.com*
Instagram: *@olegkaganwriter*

R.H. ALEXANDER lives in the Twin Cities area and is retired after a thirty-five year career as a newspaper editor and manufacturer's representative. He is married to Pamela Hill Nettleton, has seven grandchildren, and claims to learn more about truth from them than anywhere and anyone else in these strange days. He has been writing poetry since he was six and his work has been published online and in print by Train River Publishing, The Eve Poetry Group, and Witches 'N Pink. His first book *Confession from Eden* released in 2022.

RACHAEL HOLMES is a teaching assistant with a degree in Psychology. She loves to compose poetry with themes of nature and relationships, and to explore the boundary between humanity and the natural world.

Blog: *myfreshpages.wordpress.com*

ROBERT BIRKHOFER is a writer, a dreamer, and a coffee drinker. He lives in sunny Arizona with his wife and their two cats. Visit Robert's website to read more of his stories and for information on his other published works.

Blog: *themadpuppeteer.com*
Instagram: *@the_madpuppeteer*

SADIE is a 22 year old amateur artist as well as writer who has been drawing for a long time now but only recently started writing poems about life and depression expressing her feelings. She believes in the power of expression. It can heal a soul.

SARAH LICHT is a third-year college student, a writer of poems and short stories, and an avid dreamer and gamer. A Florida-native, she would much rather avoid the sunshine altogether and curl up with a good book. When she isn't writing, she can be found getting another cup of coffee, watching bad movies, or playing with her cat Lilith. In the future, she hopes to publish her own poetry collection and, even more hopefully, several novels.

Instagram: *@wordsby_sarah*

STEPHANIE LAMB began writing at a young age but primarily kept her work in private journals. In her mid-twenties she went through severe writer's block while seeking medical intervention for insomnia and anxiety. She rediscovered her voice and now writes to empower others and give a voice to the voiceless.

STEVEN BRYSON is a part-time artist who lives on the Isle of Wight with his wife and daughter. He uses his art as a way of relaxing and keeping his mental issues at bay.

Blog: *smallislandscribbler.wordpress.com*
Instagram: *@stevebrysonart*

SUSA

TARA CARIBOU is a crunchy neo-hippie who flourishes in the wilds of rural Alaska. Wrestling with OCD-related depression, persistent repetition of thoughts, and constant analysis, she allows her love of nature to drive her inspiration and peace. She has three books of poetry and photographic art published, *Fallen Star Rising, Four,* and *Euphoria in Blue.* You can find her writing and creating from the heart barefoot on the beach or wandering deep in the woods. Read more of her work on her website.

Blog: *taracaribou.com*
Instagram: *@tara_caribou*

www.ingramcontent.com/pod-product-compliance
Lightning Source LLC
LaVergne TN
LVHW090954080826
845145LV00003B/1010

* 9 7 8 1 7 3 6 0 4 1 7 4 1 *